THE
SPIRIT WORLD

✣

TIME ®
LIFE
BOOKS

Other Publications:

WEIGHT WATCHERS₈ SMART CHOICE RECIPE COLLECTION
TRUE CRIME
THE ART OF WOODWORKING
LOST CIVILIZATIONS
ECHOES OF GLORY
THE NEW FACE OF WAR
HOW THINGS WORK
WINGS OF WAR
CREATIVE EVERYDAY COOKING
COLLECTOR'S LIBRARY OF THE UNKNOWN
CLASSICS OF WORLD WAR II
TIME-LIFE LIBRARY OF CURIOUS AND UNUSUAL FACTS
AMERICAN COUNTRY
VOYAGE THROUGH THE UNIVERSE
THE THIRD REICH
THE TIME-LIFE GARDENER'S GUIDE
MYSTERIES OF THE UNKNOWN
TIME FRAME
FIX IT YOURSELF
FITNESS, HEALTH & NUTRITION
SUCCESSFUL PARENTING
HEALTHY HOME COOKING
UNDERSTANDING COMPUTERS
LIBRARY OF NATIONS
THE ENCHANTED WORLD
THE KODAK LIBRARY OF CREATIVE PHOTOGRAPHY
GREAT MEALS IN MINUTES
THE CIVIL WAR
PLANET EARTH
COLLECTOR'S LIBRARY OF THE CIVIL WAR
THE EPIC OF FLIGHT
THE GOOD COOK
WORLD WAR II
HOME REPAIR AND IMPROVEMENT
THE OLD WEST

*For information on and a full description of any of the
Time-Life Books series listed above, please call
1-800-621-7026 or write:*
Reader Information
Time-Life Customer Service
P.O. Box C-32068
Richmond, Virginia 23261-2068

This volume is one of a series that chronicles the history and culture of the Native Americans.

The Cover: Medicine Mask Dance, painted in 1850 by Canadian artist Paul Kane, depicts masked Klallam shamans near Vancouver Island, British Columbia, invoking the goodwill of supernatural forces. Almost every Native American society performed ceremonies to appease spiritual powers before undertaking any major action, such as hunting, planting, or going to war.

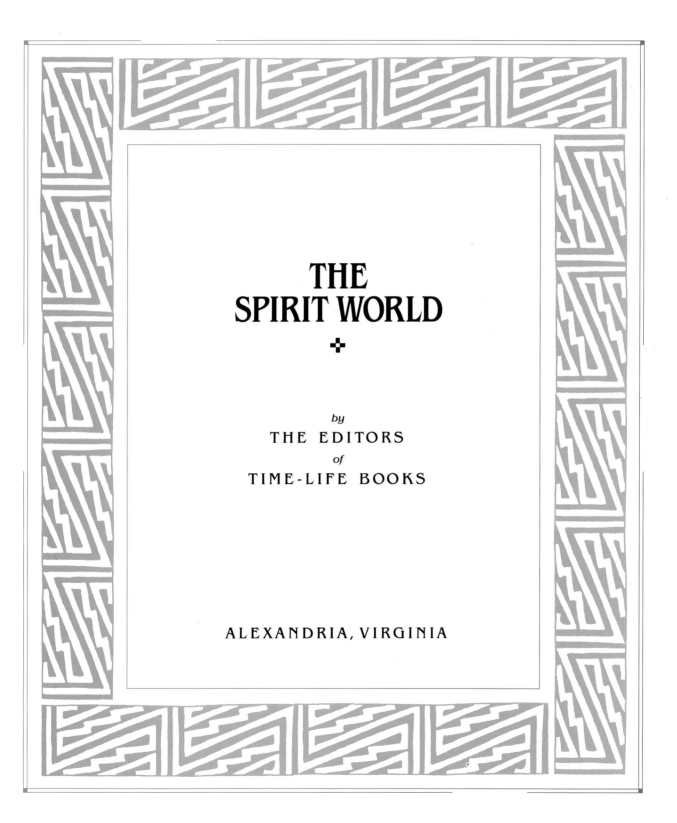

THE SPIRIT WORLD

✤

by
THE EDITORS
of
TIME-LIFE BOOKS

ALEXANDRIA, VIRGINIA

THE AMERICAN INDIANS

SERIES EDITOR: Henry Woodhead
Administrative Editor: Jane Edwin

Editorial Staff for *The Spirit World:*
Senior Art Directors: Dale Pollekoff (principal), Herbert H. Quarmby
Picture Editor: Susan V. Kelly
Text Editors: John Newton (principal), Stephen G. Hyslop
Writer: Maggie Debelius
Associate Editors/Research: Catherine Chase Tyson (principal), Robin Currie
Assistant Art Director: Susan M. Gibas
Senior Copyeditor: Ann Lee Bruen
Picture Coordinator: David Beard
Editorial Assistants: Jayne A. L. Dover, Gemma Villanueva

Special Contributors: Amy Aldrich, Tony Allan, William Barnhill, George Constable, Lee Hassig, Lydia Preston Hicks, Barbara C. Mallen, Susan Perry, David S. Thomson (text); Martha Lee Beckington, Virginia Bynum, Jocelyn G. Lindsay, Marilyn Murphy Terrell, Jennifer Veech, Anne Whittle (research); Barbara L. Klein (index).

Correspondents: Elisabeth Kraemer-Singh (Bonn), Christine Hinze (London), Christina Lieberman (New York), Maria Vincenza Aloisi (Paris), Ann Natanson (Rome). Valuable assistance was also provided by: Elizabeth Brown, Katheryn White (New York), Carolyn L. Sackett (Seattle).

General Consultants

Frederick E. Hoxie is director of the D'Arcy McNickle Center for the History of the American Indian at the Newberry Library in Chicago. Dr. Hoxie is the author of *A Final Promise: The Campaign to Assimilate the Indians 1880-1920* and other works. He has served as a history consultant to the Cheyenne River and Standing Rock Sioux tribes, Little Big Horn College archives, and the Senate Select Committee on Indian Affairs. He is a trustee of the National Museum of the American Indian in Washington, D.C.

Jay Miller is an anthropologist and adjunct professor at the Native American Educational Services in Chicago. He has been a research associate and director of the American Indian Studies Program at the University of Washington and editor and assistant director at the D'Arcy McNickle Center for the History of the American Indian at the Newberry Library. As part of his lifelong involvement with Native Americans, Dr. Miller has been tutored by the elders of many North American tribes, including the Delaware, Salish, Creek, and Tsimshian, and has participated in their rituals. He has also written numerous articles about Native Americans for professional journals and is the author of several books, among them *Shamanic Odyssey: Lushootseed Salish Journey to the Land of the Dead* and *Earthmaker and Other Tribal Stories from Native North America.*

Special Consultants

Bill Holm, retired since 1985, was for many years curator of Northwest Coast Indian art at the Burke Museum in Seattle and a professor of art history at the University of Washington. Drawing upon his longtime interest and involvement in Native American cultures, he is working on a series of acrylic paintings of the people of the Plains, Plateau, and Northwest Coast. Professor Holm has lectured widely on native Northwest arts and cultures and has published numerous books, including *Northwest Coast Indian Art: An Analysis of Form* and *Box of Daylight: Northwest Coast Indian Art.*

Alfonso Ortiz, professor of anthropology at the University of New Mexico, is the author of *The Tewa World* and numerous other books. He was a contributing editor of the two Southwest volumes of *The Handbook of North American Indians* and coeditor of *Myths and Legends of North American Indians.* Dr. Ortiz has also written dozens of articles for both scholarly and general publications. Among his professional affiliations, he was a MacArthur Foundation Fellow from 1982 to 1987.

Library of Congress Cataloging in Publication Data
The Spirit World/by the editors of Time-Life Books.
   p.   cm. — (The American Indians)
   Includes bibliographical references.
   ISBN 0-8094-9404-3
   ISBN 0-8094-9405-1 (lib. bdg.)
   1. Indians of North America—Religion and mythology.   2. Indians of North America—Rites and ceremonies. I. Time-Life Books.   II. Series.
E98.R3S723   1992   92-7592
299'.71—dc20   CIP

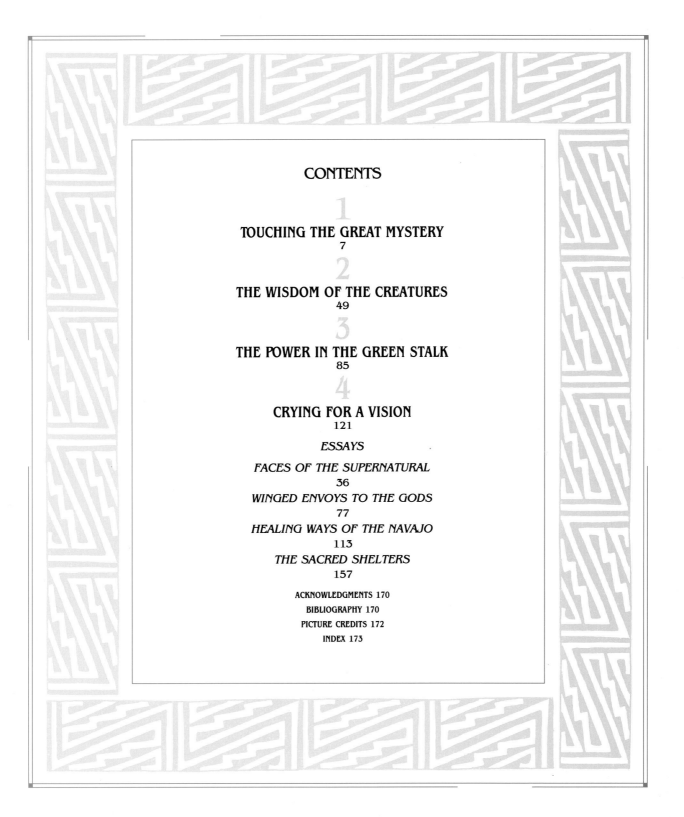

CONTENTS

1

TOUCHING THE GREAT MYSTERY

At the foot of this remote outcropping in Montana, the great Sioux chieftain and wise man Sitting Bull had a vision of victory before his forces annihilated Custer's 7th U.S. Cavalry Regiment at the Battle of the Little Bighorn in 1876. The rock remains a sacred place to Plains Indians.

In early June of 1876, Sitting Bull knew that a showdown with the United States government was near at hand. All his life, the revered spiritual leader of the Lakota nation (the Indian name for the western Sioux) had fought to save his people's ancestral hunting grounds from the encroachment of the whites. And now the government, as a preliminary step to yet another land grab and in violation of an existing treaty, had dispatched federal troops to the Powder River country of central Montana to force the Sioux back onto the reservation that had been set aside for them in South Dakota.

The 45-year-old chief scrubbed the war paint from his face and bound the stem of his ceremonial pipe with sprigs of fresh-picked sage. Accompanied by three witnesses, he climbed to the top of a lonely butte to seek guidance and inspiration from Wakan Tanka, the Great Mystery. Below him, along the banks of Rosebud Creek, the tipis of 15,000 Sioux and their Cheyenne and Arapaho allies stretched for nearly three miles.

"Let good men on earth have more power," Sitting Bull prayed. "Let them be of good heart, so that all Sioux people may get along well and be happy." Then he vowed to perform the Sun Dance, which was the most holy of Sioux rituals.

In a special camp beside the Rosebud, Sitting Bull offered Wakan Tanka a "scarlet blanket," 50 pellets of his flesh, cut out of each arm from wrist to shoulder with a needle-pointed awl and a sharp knife. Then he danced, all day, all night, and part of the next day, until finally he fainted from exhaustion. In his disembodied state, Sitting Bull received a vision, a dream of soldiers in defeat, of many white soldiers falling "like grasshoppers" into the Indians' camp.

The news of Sitting Bull's vision spread like a brush fire through the Indian camps, bolstering the resolve of the warriors. Not long afterward, on a ridge above a river known to the Indians as the Greasy Grass, the Sioux and their allies destroyed a force of United States cavalrymen led by Lieutenant Colonel George Armstrong Custer. Ever since, Sitting Bull and the Battle of the Little Bighorn, as the white men called the historic clash, have been inseparably linked in the American consciousness. But contrary to popular notion, the great chief played no role in the actual fighting. He had done his work at the Sun Dance; he had passed the power of Wakan Tanka to his warriors.

Sitting Bull's encounter with the spirit world came near the end of a tragic struggle that finally concluded with the defeat of an Indian culture. Although his people did not prevail in their conflict with the government, the chief's dream beside the Rosebud would be celebrated as one of the enduring and uplifting episodes in the chronicles of the American Indians. In another sense, however—in an Indian sense—a meeting with the Great Spirit was far from unique. Sitting Bull's vision represented an epic example of the kind of personal revelation experienced by countless followers of Indian faith. In the Indians' world, such revelations are not reserved solely for warriors or great chiefs in times of crisis. Communication with mysterious powers is available to all;

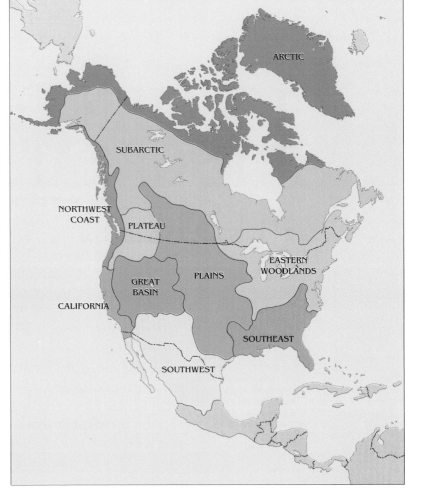

dreams and visions serve as messages or instructions that any of the faithful may expect to receive as gifts from an unseen power. Dreams exist for ordinary people to illuminate the path of the individual's life, as guidebooks for living, for making one's way through the day. In the world of the Indians, the dream is real.

For as far back as they can travel along the chain of memory, the American Indians have dwelled in a world filled with spirits. From time immemorial, the birds have carried messages to the gods beyond the clouds, the rivers have sung, and the rocks have talked. This spiritual universe is prismatic in its complexity. There is no single Native American religion, but rather as many religions as there are Indian peoples. Although tribes that share common geography and walks of life, such as the

The tales and legends of North American Indians have varied markedly by region, reflecting the local climate, geography, and wildlife. The dwellers of the eastern woodlands told stories of forest animals—wolves, rabbit, and deer. Indians living on the coasts populate their tales with seabirds, fish, and killer whales. These various cultural regions are indicated on the map above, which also shows the original locations of the Indian tribes discussed in this volume.

Men of the Apache tribe listen to a tale told by a storyteller (second from right). All Indian groups used the spoken word to pass along knowledge of tribal history from generation to generation, making storytelling an integral part of the Indians' spiritual life.

seafaring peoples of the Northwest Coast or the buffalo hunters of the Great Plains, tend to have similar sacred beliefs, each Indian community follows its own life path in a spiritual realm informed not only by the tribe's ancestral homelands, but the waters upon them, the skies above them, and the creatures that inhabit them.

The roots of these belief systems reach back millions of years. Collectively, they form a rich and diverse trove of legends, rites, and rituals, the core of which remains intact today—despite the fact that the United States government assumed by force billions of acres of Indian land and, for nearly 60 years, from 1880 to 1934, outlawed many Indian sacred practices in an effort to force the assimilation of Native Americans.

These diverse Indian religions have a great deal in common, including the fact that the word *religion,* though used for convenience, inadequately defines them. In truth, the Indian equivalent of the word does not appear in any of the hundreds of languages and thousands of dialects spoken in North America. The word implies that the various aspects of life can be segmented into the sacred and the secular—a notion unfathomable to a Native American. According to traditional Indian thinking, there is nothing that can be seen or touched, living or inanimate, that does not have a spirit. Spirituality and ordinary life are as interconnected as the strands of a tightly woven rug. As John Lame Deer, a Miniconjou

Sioux, explains: "We Indians live in a world of symbols where the spiritual and the commonplace are one. To you, symbols are just words, spoken or written in a book. To us, they are a part of nature, part of ourselves—the earth, the sun, the wind and the rain, stones, trees, animals, even little insects like ants and grasshoppers. We try to understand them not with the head but with the heart, and we need no more than a hint to give us the meaning."

A pipe or a pair of moccasins that may appear quaint or mundane to a non-Indian's eyes may have enormous spiritual significance to an Indian. A carving or a painting that the non-Indian observer considers ornamental art may be part of a sacred process. A dance that might be viewed as purely recreational could have a profound spiritual meaning. "The purpose of our ceremonies is not entertainment, but attainment," a Tewa Indian once informed an Anglo visitor, "the attainment of the Balanced Life. Our dramas, our songs, and our dances are not performed for fun as they might be in the white man's world; they are more than that; they are the very essence of our lives."

The cycles that are dominant in the natural world—the path of the sun moving across the sky, the change of the seasons, the germination of seeds, and the birth, growth, and death of all creatures—evolve in an orderly fashion, day after day, year after year, generation after generation, under the control of unseen forces. Mysterious powers abide in all things found in the natural world—the flora, the fauna, the very earth itself. Everything that exists possesses a soul, and all of these souls are mutually dependent. Or, as one old Sioux man explained: "All living things are tied together with a common navel cord." Native Americans believe that if they act in accordance with sacred tradition, they maintain harmony between humans and other elements of the natural world. If they violate the sacred ways, however, the orderly workings of the natural world are thrown out of kilter, and the imbalance may cause bad things to happen—sickness, accident, disaster.

Many Indian peoples have traditionally prayed to the soul of the game or fish that has been killed for sustenance. They believe that such creatures have intentionally sacrificed themselves for the benefit of the Indians, and they beg the animals to forgive them for taking their lives. The sense of mutual dependence and respect afforded by many tribes to the natural world extends even to the soil, which for its part has granted sustenance in the form of crops. Barre Toelken, a scholar who lived with several Native American communities, tells of some Pueblo Indian farm-

Two elaborately costumed figures of the Menominee Indians represent a husband (right) and wife. To help a marriage prosper, the dolls were tied face to face and love medicines placed in the breast of each. Such representations were believed to have the power to summon supernatural forces; similar figures were used to help bring rain, ensure good crops, provide a plentiful catch of fish, or otherwise influence the future.

ers who rejected a white agricultural extension agent's advice to use a steel plow to prepare their fields for spring planting. The Indian custom had been to use a digging stick, and they planted not in rows but in a spiral starting at the center of the field and spreading outward. To the extension agent, the use of the plow was a simple technical improvement that would lead to a higher crop yield. To the Indians, however, it was a religious issue: They believed that in springtime the ground is pregnant and in need of gentle treatment, just like a pregnant woman. Making furrows with a hard instrument would injure the earth and violate the bond of trust between Indians and the land.

In the same manner as sacred tradition has taught respect for the natural world, so has it reinforced the idea of an individual's responsibility to others and to the tribe at large. In the world of the Indians, however, Christian notions of good and evil have been viewed in terms of balance and imbalance, harmony and disharmony. Indeed, in times past, the ideals of behavior that were taught by the elders to promote harmony— unselfishness, patience, forgiveness—were necessary for the very survival of the community in a harsh and variable wilderness. Notions of personal success and status also hinge on spirituality. Good fortune comes to those who acquire sacred knowledge. Only with the help of supernatural forces can an Indian hunt well, farm well, bring up children well, and if necessary, fight well.

Traditionally, the sacred ways of the Indians have no provision for a hell that may await a sinner, nor did religion emphasize punishment for misdeeds. A child of the tribe grew up in a world of spirituality, one relatively free of coercion or threat. Youngsters learned by example, and religion came as easily as taking a breath.

"The Indian loved to worship," wrote Luther Standing Bear, a Sioux who was born in 1868. "From birth to death, he revered his surroundings. He considered himself born in the luxurious lap of Mother Earth, and no place was to him humble. There was nothing between him and the Big Holy (Wakan Tanka). The contact was immediate and personal, and the blessings of Wakan Tanka flowed over the Indian like rain showered from the sky. Wakan Tanka was not aloof, apart, and ever seeking to quell evil forces. He did not punish the animals and the birds, and likewise, he did not punish man. He was not a punishing god. For there was never a question as to the supremacy of an evil power over and above the power of Good. There was but one ruling power, and that was Good."

Many non-Indians who became acquainted with tribes in times past

A DANCE OF RENEWAL

The hoop dance, a tradition among the Plains Indians, is a celebration of the annual rebirth of nature that occurs every springtime. The spiritual significance of the dance begins with the hoops themselves; these are made of either wood or reeds and total 28 in number, each one of them representing a day in the lunar cycle. The Sioux musician and dancer Kevin Locke, shown here performing various elements of the dance, explains that the hoops are symbolic of the "great hoop of life, where the sky meets the earth, and all of the hoops that exist within that sphere."

By skillfully twirling the hoops, the dancer creates visual stories that explain the way in which all natural things are connected, yet grow and change individually. He brings to mind the eagle *(center),* the great bird that "represents that aspect of us that does not originate from the earth, this world of dust, but from the realms on high—the spiritual worlds of God." During another portion of the dance, he emulates a lowly caterpillar that turns into a beautiful butterfly *(below).*

The conclusion of the performance consists of a dramatic movement

known as the Hoop of Many Hoops *(top),* which symbolizes the sun, the moon, the earth—all light, all life, and the human spirit reaching toward the realization that everything is interconnected. The Hoop of Many Hoops, says Locke, is also a depiction of the old Sioux prophecy that one day in the future all peoples, friends and enemies alike, shall sit down together in peace, united in a single great circle by the common bond of their humanity.

were impressed by the Indian way of life. George Catlin, the American painter and adventurer who traveled among some 48 tribes west of the Mississippi River in the 1830s, often expressed admiration for the Indians' generosity and sense of fairness. "I love a people who are honest without laws, who have no jails and no poorhouses," he wrote. "I love a people who keep the Commandments without ever having read them or heard them preached, who never take the name of God in vain, and who are free from religious animosities."

For some tribes, the powers that control the universe and all its beings take the form of deities. In other cultures, the powers have no definite shape or form but are simply mystic energies. The Iroquois of central New York and the Lake Ontario region of Canada call this supernatural force the Orenda power. The Algonquin tribes of the northeast woodlands call it Manitou. A member of the Osage tribe, a Prairie people related to the Sioux, attempted to explain the Sioux's Great Spirit, Wakan. "All life is Wakan. So also is everything that exhibits power, whether in action, as the winds and drifting clouds, or in passive endurance, as the boulder by the wayside. Even the commonest sticks and stones have a spiritual essence that must be reverenced as a manifestation of the all-pervading mysterious power that fills the universe."

To the Inuit, or Eskimo people, who reside in the ice-covered Baffin Bay region of northern Canada, this power is known as Sila. One of the Inuit elders defined it as "supporting the world and the weather and all life on earth; a spirit so mighty that what it says to humankind is not through common words, but by storm and snow and rain and the fury of the sea; all the forces of nature that people fear. But Sila has also another way of communicating—by sunlight and the calm of the sea, and little children innocently at play, themselves understanding nothing. When all is well, Sila sends no message, but withdraws into endless nothingness. So Sila remains as long as we do not abuse life, but act with reverence toward our daily food. No one has seen Sila; this spirit is at once among us and unspeakably far away."

Each Native American community has its individual ways of harnessing the powers. Before undertaking an important action, such as planting seeds, beginning a hunt, or going off to war, a large number of tribes performed special protective rituals. They might enact other rites designed to cure illness or signal the passage into adulthood of adolescent

HOPI SNAKE PRIEST

CHEROKEE MEDICINE MAN NAMED SWIMMER

A gallery of religious leaders from eight different tribes is shown in the early-20th-century photographs above and on the following pages. Revered for their power to elicit help from the spirit world, these sacred healers conducted rituals to cure the sick, influence the future, and ensure good fortune in a variety of endeavors.

boys and girls. Following a birth, a mother and father and their newborn might go into seclusion for a period of time so that rituals could be performed to bestow good health on the baby. An Inuit mother might sew a hawk's wing on the clothing of her little boy to give him speed, a fox's tail to impart cunning, or a seabird's skin for luck in fishing. A Kwakiutl (Kwakwaka'wakw) mother might place a raccoon's paw on her baby's right hand in the hope of producing a hard worker, or perhaps a squirrel's foot to make a good climber. Members of Plains and woodlands communities go off to a hilltop and fast to the point of exhaustion in order to seek a guiding vision from a spirit.

In the majority of Native American communities there are certain individuals who devote their lives to acquiring knowledge about the powers. The first Europeans to observe these Indians at work were French trappers in Canada who, upon noting that healing was one of their functions, labeled them *médecins* (doctors). Thereafter, the name "medicine men" became attached to them, although nowadays they are often called priests, or shamans, a word that originally described the mystic healers of Siberia. These sacred practitioners attempt to maintain a proper balance between the tribe and the spirit world, thus ensuring success in hunting or planting, or in preventing sickness and curing disease. Although sha-

NOOTKA FEMALE SHAMAN BRAVE BUFFALO, SIOUX MEDICINE MAN

mans are generally male, a few Indian communities have postmenopausal females serving in the role. (Women of childbearing age are universally excluded from shamanism because menstrual blood is thought to possess special power of its own; it is subject to many taboos for some tribes; others see it as a symbol of potential fecundity.)

One of the major responsibilities of these keepers-of-knowledge in many communities has been to pass down from generation to generation the tribe's ancient legends—what Luther Standing Bear called the "libraries of our people." In these tales, the boundaries between mortals and immortals, animals and humans, past and present, and space and time drift and blur. Although some Indian storytellers may have sand drawings, sacred birch-bark scrolls, or ancient paintings on rocks or animal hides to help them recall details, they have always relied primarily on the strength of their own memories.

Almost all Native American communities refer to themselves in their own language by an expression that means "the People." A tribe's oral tradition—especially the part of it that describes the community's origin—serves as the foundation of the People's sacred way. These spiritual charters provide the terms by which the People perceive reality and grapple with the basic questions concerning the human condition, namely, Where

OLD SOPHIE, KAROK MEDICINE WOMAN

OWL WOMAN, PAPAGO MEDICINE WOMAN

do we come from? and Where are we going? The stories explain how the world came into being or how it has been transformed; they teach the People guidelines of behavior and provide them with the tools of survival, such as the ability to hunt certain animals, plant certain crops, or perform certain ceremonies and prayers.

Exactly how long these creation legends have existed is unknown. Because they share certain similarities with the stories of Eurasia and Siberia, it is possible that the nomadic ancestors of the Indians brought elements of the tales with them from the Old World across the Siberian-Alaskan land bridge into North America. As the migrants worked their way south and east, they embroidered the tales to reflect elements of the surrounding environment and their own changing tribal histories: Gradually, the sharing of stories and the collective experience among tribes living in particular regions of North America gave rise to regional tales that shared similar characteristics. From the northeastern forest dwellers came versions of the stories featuring the Arctic hare, the wolf, and the cedar tree; from the agricultural southerners, legends of corn maidens and sacred mountains; and from the coastal peoples, tales of aquatic animals, seabirds, and ocean monsters.

The tales have been told most frequently around a fire on a winter

TLINGIT SHAMAN   **MOVES SLOWLY, MANDAN CORN PRIEST**

night. At times, the stories are accompanied by rhythmic chanting or prayers uttered in an archaic language that is often incomprehensible to the audience. But the words are spoken nonetheless because they carry special power. A Netsilik Inuit has described the ancient utterances as "thoughts, sung out with the breath when people are moved by great forces and ordinary language no longer suffices."

In some tribes, the tales are preceded by special rites. The Maidu, who lived along the eastern tributaries of the Sacramento River in present-day northern California, required the audience to lie down on their backs, the better to promote quiet and attentiveness. The Cheyenne, an Algonquian-speaking people who migrated from the territory that is now Minnesota to the Great Plains, specify that the narrator introduce the tale by smoothing the ground and passing his hands over his body in brushing motions. In other cultures, the listeners must give the storyteller a gift before the story can begin.

The Seneca of the Northeast begin their tales with the phrase, "When the world was new . . ." The Pima and Papago (O'odom) of the Southwest often begin their stories with "They say it happened long ago . . ." Still other tribes start with words that trigger a liturgical response. For example, the Zuni, an agricultural Pueblo people of the Southwest, begin their stories with the phrase, "Now we are taking it up," to which the audience replies, "Yes, indeed." The narrator then says, "Now it begins to be made." After the storyteller has finished, some California Indians order the tale back to its cave, as if it were alive.

In general, the tales found in the oral tradition involve the workings of supernatural powers and the spirits of clever animals, such as ravens, raccoon, fox, beaver, blue jays, and spiders, who speak the language of the People. These animals may play the role of a helper, a meddler, or a combination of the two. Among all the creatures that appear in stories that recount the origin of a tribe, none appears more frequently than the coyote, an animal Indians all across western North America universally respect for its supreme cunning and remarkable ability to survive in all kinds of environments—on the prairie, in the woodland, in the mountains, and in the desert.

Recurring themes include the idea of Mother Earth as life host, the relationship of reciprocity that exists between human beings and animals, and the Indians' dependence on animals as teachers. The plots are often complex, take numerous twists and turns, and commonly include humor. But any comic elements never detract from the story's sacred purpose. "They are not funny stories," a Navajo man once said of his people's oral histories. "Many things about the story are funny, but the story is not funny. If my children hear the stories, they will grow up to be good people; if they do not hear them, they will turn out bad."

In contrast to the biblical book of Genesis, in which God creates man in his own image and gives him dominion over all other creatures, the Native American legends reflect the view that human beings are no more important than any other thing, whether alive or inanimate. In the eye of the Creator, they believe, man and woman, plant and animal, water and stone, are all equal, and they share the earth as partners—even as family. "We Indians think of the earth and the whole universe as a never-ending circle, and in this circle, man is just another animal," explains Jenny Leading Cloud of the Rosebud Indian Reservation. "The buffalo and the coyote are our brothers; the birds, our cousins. We end our prayers with the words *all my relations*—and that includes everything that grows, crawls, runs, creeps, hops, and flies."

The Crow Indians believe that the earth was created by a coyote. A people renowned for their muscular build, handsome features, and shoulder-length black hair, the Crows were hard-riding buffalo hunters and fierce warriors who claimed an ancestral homeland in present-day

A LIFE UNCHANGED BY TIME

For thousands of years, the Karok, the Yurok, and the Hupa peoples have lived in the same remote corner of the Klamath River valley in northern California, sealed off from outsiders by the Cascade Range to the east and the Pacific Ocean to the west. Isolated in this natural cul-de-sac of spectacular beauty and bountiful resources, the three neighboring tribes developed similar lifestyles—fishing for salmon, hunting deer, gathering acorns, and making finely twined basketry—despite the fact that they all speak different languages.

At the core of each culture lies an abiding reverence for the land, especially for the sacred mountains and oak trees. During an autumn ceremony called the White Deerskin Dance, shamans carry out secret rites to renew nature and perpetuate the well-being of the community. The tribes also share several common prayer sites, among them Doctor Rock, where medicine men and women often go as part of their spiritual training. "Without our mountain," one Karok has said, "the whole tribe will crumble."

In former times, the tribes traveled the river highways in dugout canoes fashioned by the Yurok out of the giant redwood trees that grow in their homeland on the lower Klamath. The eight-foot-long canoe below, which was crafted by Axel Lindgren, a fifth-generation Yurok, bears traditional carved representations of human lungs, kidneys, and heart. "The canoe itself," explains Lindgren, "is a symbol of the continuation of life."

Hupa men wearing headdresses decorated with wolf skins dance on several dugout canoes in the Trinity River. The Boat Dance was part of their festival to renew nature in the year 1898.

The Karok believe this cone-shaped mountain, called Aheuich, at the confluence of the Klamath and Salmon rivers to be the center of the earth. Downriver from this spot, they hold their ritual to honor the first salmon catch in the spring, in addition to their World Renewal ceremony in the fall.

The lives of the Karok, Yurok, and Hupas have always revolved around the seasonal bounty offered by the thick forest and the fast-flowing rivers of their northern California homeland. Each spring, the salmon make their spawning runs, and men still fish from the same rocky promontories that their great-great-grandfathers used.

Autumn provides acorns, the other traditional staple, which are gathered in the oak groves along the rivers. The women pound the shelled acorns into flour, which they soak in water to remove the bitter tannin. The acorn flour is then mixed with fresh water in tightly woven baskets and cooked with hot stones until it becomes a soup.

Material for the baskets comes from the forests and riverbanks. Using willow roots, alder bark, fern stems, and bear grass, the women weave flat-bottomed, watertight containers traditionally used for cooking, and deep, conical ones for gathering and storing dried food. Most of the baskets are ornamented with squares, diamonds, and zigzags—designs that are also worked into the woven caps worn by the women on ceremonial occasions.

Standing on a scaffold of slender poles, a Karok Indian fishes the Klamath River with a traditional dip net in this photograph taken in the late 19th century. It was not uncommon for a single household to catch sufficient fish in one season to feed the family for the entire year.

A Yurok woman prepares acorns for soup in a woven bowl similar to the one shown at right, which contains both shelled and un-shelled acorns and a stone pestle. She wears a basketry hat like the one at far right.

Wyoming and in Montana, near the magnificent Bighorn Mountains. They were the bitter rivals of the Sioux and the Blackfeet, whom they contested regularly for horses, hunting grounds, and fame.

In the beginning, according to the Crow tale, Old Man Coyote stood alone, gazing out on an endless expanse of water. In time, two red-eyed ducks paddled by, and Old Man Coyote eagerly asked them if they had seen anything else during their travels. The ducks replied that they had seen nothing, but suggested that perhaps something existed underneath the waters. His curiosity piqued, Old Man Coyote asked them to have a look. So one of the ducks dove to the bottom, only to return with nothing. Old Man Coyote appealed to him to try again. This time, the duck resurfaced with a small root in his bill. Then he dove a third time and brought up a lump of mud.

"Well, my younger brothers," Old Man Coyote announced, "this is something we can build on." Old Man Coyote blew on the mud until it expanded into an island. He blew one more time, and the island grew into the earth.

"It would be nicer if it were not so empty," suggested one of the ducks. To please them, Old Man Coyote then made the grass, the trees, and all the plants out of the root that the duck had plucked from beneath the waters. The ducks and the coyote admired the brown prairie that now lay before them, but eventually they decided that it was too flat. So Old Man Coyote shifted the earth around to form rivers, canyons, and mountains.

"This is perfect," exclaimed the ducks happily. "Who could imagine anything more?"

Nevertheless, Old Man Coyote was not entirely satisfied with what he had created. "This is very beautiful," he conceded. "But I am lonely and bored. We need companions."

So Old Man Coyote scooped up some of the earth and shaped it into men. After finishing that task, he molded male ducks of all varieties. Old Man Coyote was extremely pleased with his handiwork until he realized that he had forgotten something.

"If there were women, the men would be content, and they could multiply and grow strong," he said. So he scooped up another handful of dirt and made women and female ducks.

Made by Lakota women, a turtle-shaped pouch of leather, beads, and coins holds an umbilical cord. Such amulets were hung from a baby's cradleboard, then kept as a charm against evil and misfortune.

Then, one day while Old Man Coyote was walking about the earth, he encountered another coyote. ''Why younger brother, what a wonderful surprise!'' he said. ''Where did you come from?''

''Well, my elder brother, I don't know. I exist. That is all. Here I am. Shirape, I call myself.'' The two coyotes traveled together across the land. Shirape suggested that Old Man Coyote make some other animals besides ducks. Old Man Coyote agreed and made them by pronouncing different animal names, such as buffalo, deer, elk, antelope, and bear. After a while, he created the drum, songs, and dancing. When the bear threatened the other animals with his claws, Old Man Coyote banished him to a den where he had to sleep all winter long.

Meanwhile, the people were in a miserable state. One day, Shirape suggested to Old Man Coyote that he should give them tools to work with, tipis to live in, and fire to cook by and warm themselves. Shirape also suggested giving them bows and arrows and spears so that they could hunt better. ''Why shouldn't the animals have bows and arrows too?'' Old Man Coyote inquired.

''Don't you see?'' Shirape replied. ''The animals are swift. They already have big claws, teeth, and powerful horns. The people are slow. Their teeth and nails are not very strong. If the animals had weapons, how could the people survive?''

Old Man Coyote gave the people weapons, but Shirape remained dissatisfied. ''There is only one language,'' he complained. ''You cannot fight somebody who speaks your language. There should be enmity. There should be war.''

''What are wars good for?'' asked Old Man Coyote.

''Oh, my respected elder brother,'' Shirape replied. ''Sometimes you are not thinking. War is a good thing. Say you are a warrior. You paint yourself with vermilion. You wear a fine war shirt. You sing war songs. You have war honors. You look at the good-looking young girls. You look at the young women whose husbands have no war honors. They look back at you. You go on the warpath. You steal the enemy's horses. You steal his women and maidens. You count coup, do brave deeds. You are rich. You have gifts to give away. They sing songs honoring you. You have many loves. And by and by, you become a chief.'' So Old Man Coyote divided the people into tribes, giving them different languages. Then there was war, then there was horse stealing, then there was counting coup, then there were songs of honor.

That the great world in all its complexity could stem from the simple act of an animal retrieving a bit of earth from the depths was a miracle celebrated in the legends of a large number of Native American peoples. Among the Plains Indians, the animal is usually a muskrat; among California Indians, a turtle or some kind of waterfowl; and among the Inuit people of the Far North, a raven armed with a spear.

According to the Seneca of New York State, several creatures worked in concert to fabricate the earth. The Seneca tale relates that long ago, at a time when the world was nothing but water, the wife of the great chief who ruled in the sky fell from her home in heaven and plummeted toward the abyss. Looking up, waterfowl saw her coming and kindly joined their bodies together in order to cushion her fall. As time passed, the woman became too heavy for the waterfowl to hold, so they persuaded a frog to dive beneath the ocean and return with the dirt needed to make a landmass. Then, they enlisted the help of a turtle and spread the dirt on the animal's carapace, where it expanded and deepened until it was able to accommodate all the creatures that were produced thereafter.

Found in Utah and dating back perhaps 3,000 years, this rock painting may represent a shaman performing a ritual with his spirit helper, a horned serpent. Indians of the Southwest have considered snakes sacred creatures that serve as messengers to the underworld and guardians of springs.

In this, as in many Native American tales of creation, great things take place when a spirit or power associated with the sky comes down to earth. The Tsimshian, a fishing and foraging people of the rugged British Columbia coast, relate a story that honors the raven for bringing light from heaven to illuminate the world below. When the earth was young and still shrouded in twilight, the tale begins, the chief of the sky gave one of the youth of heaven the skin of a raven, which the boy donned in order to fly about the world. Skirting the earth, Raven took pity on its people, whom he observed fumbling about in the twilight. He knew that there was light in heaven, and he made up his mind to bring it to the world.

To steal daylight from the chief of the sky, however, Raven had to assume an elaborate disguise. Ascending to his home in heaven, he transformed himself into a cedar leaf and dropped into a stream. There, the chief's daughter later stopped for a drink of fresh water and unwittingly swallowed him. Impregnated by this action, she soon gave birth to Raven. The precocious infant insisted on playing with a magic toy—the box that held the daylight. His doting grandfather, the chief, could deny the boy nothing and gave him the box. The boy played with the box for four days in the great house in the sky. Then, when the chief was not looking, the boy put on his raven skin and flew down to the earth, carrying the box of daylight under one wing.

After alighting on a tree near a river, Raven, who was always insatiably hungry, called to the people who were fishing in the twilight to bring him some of their catch. But they only ignored him. Furious, Raven smashed the box on the rocks that lay below the tree. There was a blinding flash of light, and instantly, the world was transformed. Dawn arrived. And so it has ever since.

Other Indian tales of creation portray the sky as a great source of power and enlightenment, but one that must first be wedded to the earth in order to bring benefits. Zuni legend asserts that at the dawn of time, Mother Earth and Father Sky lay together in the primordial waters in a fertile embrace. Growing large with her offspring, Mother Earth then separated herself from Father Sky and slid beneath the waters. In a similar story told by the Luiseno people of coastal California, life began when formless energies that were male and female drifted close to each other in the endless void. The female spoke first, saying, "I am that which stretches out flat." The male replied, "I am that which arches over everything." After this brief introduction, they made love and produced the "thoughts" of all that was to come.

According to the oral tradition of the Okanagon—a people inhabiting the sagebrush flats of a Columbia River tributary—a mysterious creator, known as the chief of the spirits, formed the earth out of a woman. "You will be the mother of all people," the chief told the earth, and as such, her spirit lives on. As the tale relates, "the soil is her flesh, the rocks are

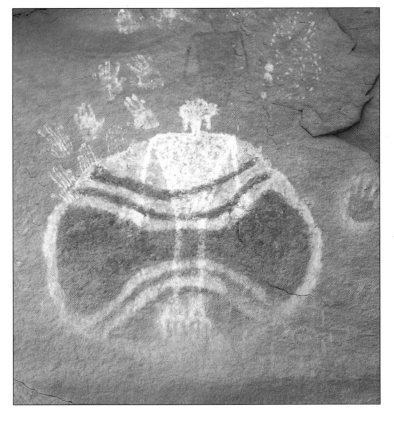

White hand prints border another ancient Utah rock painting that shows a human figure covered by a shield, a design calculated to ward off harm. The hand prints were applied as generations of pilgrims, in accordance with Indian custom, left evidence of their visits to this holy spot hoping that it would be noted by the supernatural powers.

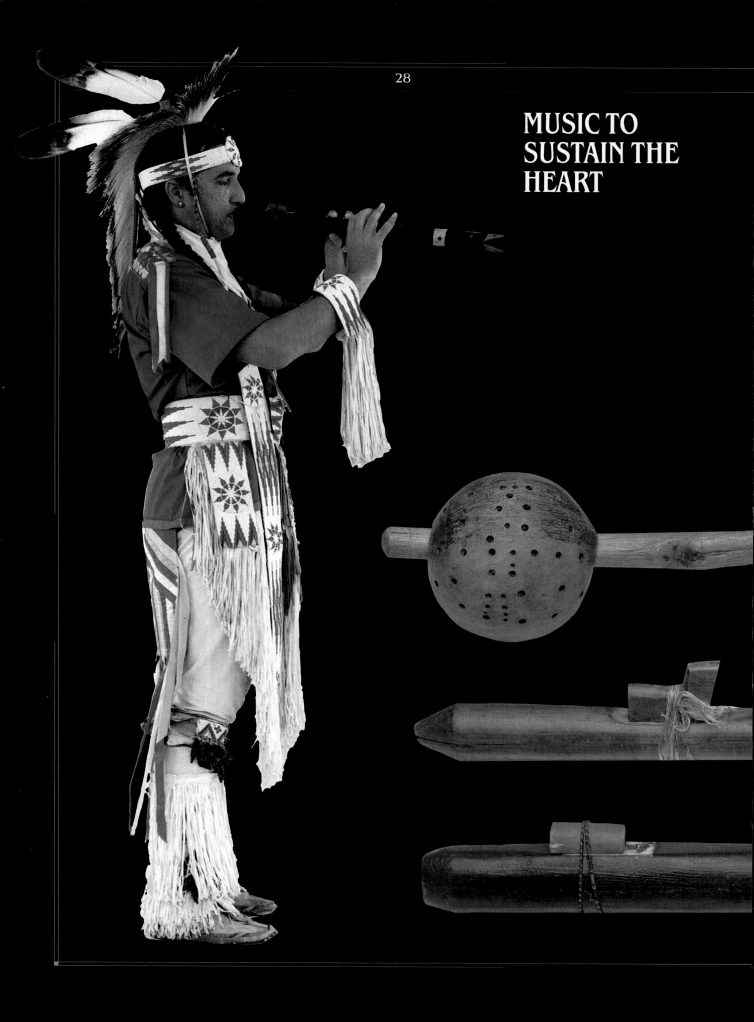

MUSIC TO SUSTAIN THE HEART

The sometimes haunting and frequently complex rhythms of traditional Native American music imitate the lifegiving processes of nature and celebrate the wholeness of the universe. In the words of the Sioux performer Kevin Locke, pictured at left, just as the powerful thunderstorms that come in the spring and summer make it possible for the prairies of the Great Plains to flourish and bloom, so true Indian music "nurtures and sustains the soil of the human heart."

Locke makes his music with the drum, the flute, and the rattle shown below, along with his singing voice. In order to explain the underlying meaning of the music he is creating, he describes the instruments as "counterpoints to the powerful, elemental forces of the thunderstorm." The beat of the drum is the thunder that "shakes the human heart out of its slough of despondency." The melodies of the flute (its six holes representing the four cardinal directions, along with the earth and the sky), are the "wind that purifies and breathes life into the heart." The sound of the rattle represents refreshing rain, and the voice is the lightning whose jagged streaks "illuminate the heart and charge it with energy and enlightenment."

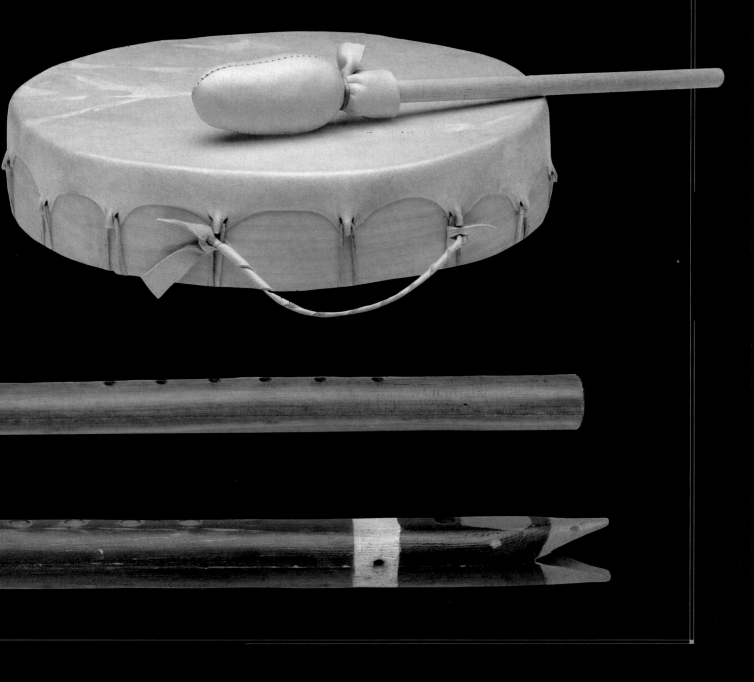

Exquisite carvings on a pair of small spindle whorls, used by women of the Salish tribes of the Pacific Northwest to keep wool from slipping off a spindle while being spun, indicate how religion informed even the most mundane tasks. The whorl at top bears the image of a sacred thunderbird with a whale in its talons, the bottom one a human figure with prominent ribs that was a typical design employed to represent shamans.

her bones, the wind her breath, trees and grass her hair. She lives spread out, and we live on her. Whenever she moves, we have an earthquake.''

Within the lands of every tribe are certain sacred places—mountains, lakes, woodlands, or canyons—that are believed to harbor extraordinary power. These revered landmarks figure prominently in the legends of many Indian peoples. The creation stories of the Navajo, for example, describe the formation of the four distinctive peaks or mountain chains that border their ancestral homeland at each quarter in the present-day Four Corners region, where the states of Utah, Colorado, Arizona, and New Mexico converge. According to one Navajo legend, First Man and First Woman created those sacred mountains from soil that First Man had stored along with other magical substances in his medicine bundle. The couple then fastened down Blanca Peak in the east with a bolt of white lightning and covered it with a blanket of daylight. They pinned Mount Taylor in the south with a stone knife and draped it in blue. They fastened the San Francisco Peaks in the west with a sunbeam and cloaked them with yellow. And they tied down Hesperus Peak in the north with a rainbow and shrouded it in darkness. From that time forward, the Navajo associated each direction with a special color and power—white for the lightning to the east, blue for the sky to the south, yellow for the sun to the west, and black for the storm clouds to the north.

Many other groups have attributed specific powers to the four directions and their related colors. The Beaver people (now called the Dunneza) of central Alberta tell of a creator named Yagesati who charted the directions by drawing a cross upon the primeval waters. Through the center of the cross, he thrust a pole that led to the upper world above and the lower world below. Then Yagesati moved in a great circle around the pole, assigning each cardinal direction a color, a time of day, a season, a sex, a stage of life, and a quality. The east he colored the red of the dawn, for the first flush of spring and the blood of birth; East was masculine, potent, and benevolent. Yagesati colored the south a dazzling yellow for the high sun, for the warmth of summer and the profusion of growing things; South was female, fertile, and kind. Yagesati next moved to the west and painted it the red of dusk, for the setting sun, for the chill of dusk and autumn; West was a dangerous female, who would lead people to death. At last, Yagesati reached the home of the moon at its zenith, the north. He colored it white for snow, for winter and its icy blasts; North represented a dangerous male and the

Attired in fantastic dress, Zuni dancers prepare for the crowning ritual of their south-western community's religious year. Held every December and called the Shalako, the elaborate ceremony is designed to reenact Zuni history and both honor the dead and propitiate the spirit world. The traditional costumes feature gargoyles that sprout long, black, bird beaks, and eagle-feather headdresses topped by buffalo horns.

trials of puberty, when one stage of existence ended and another began.

Eventually, a boy named Swan was born into the universe Yagesati charted. At the age of 13, the time of puberty, Swan set out on his first hunting trip in the depths of winter, reluctantly taking along his stepmother. The boy soon spotted a rabbit and shot it. But before Swan could grab his prey, the stepmother—an evil woman—snatched the kicking animal and placed it between her thighs, where the rabbit scratched her. Later, she showed the wounds to Swan's father and claimed that the boy had attempted to have intercourse with her.

In horror, the father took Swan to a distant island and abandoned him. Frightened and hungry, the boy cried himself to sleep and soon began to dream. In his dream, he heard a voice instructing him to pour the resin of the pine tree on some nearby rocks. The next morning, having done as the voice commanded, Swan found birds mired in the pitch. In this way, he obtained food to survive the winter.

In the springtime, the father returned to the island in order to collect his son's remains. But while his father was preoccupied searching for the bones, Swan stole his canoe and paddled home. There, he shot his stepmother with a blazing arrow that singed the flesh from her bones. Henceforth, Swan became known as Saya, or sun. Traveling the rim of the world, Saya tracked down the fearsome animals inhabiting that realm and transformed them into the game animals that the Beaver people would come to depend on. And so Saya became the first shaman. In time, every Beaver child who reached the age of 13 would be called on to make a journey symbolic of Swan's quest, entering a trance and confronting the fearsome animals. Strengthened by the ordeal, the youngster would return to the present world and proceed to adulthood, following the course of the sun around the rim of reality until death beckoned in the west.

Here as in other Native American rituals and stories, death is seen not as an enigma or an end but as part of nature's cycle—a stage like puberty that all creatures must pass through to complete the round of life. Even spirits meet with death in the legends. Indeed, spirits in animal or human form often invite death as a way of providing for those who depend on them. The Penobscot, an Algonquian-speaking people of northern Maine, have preserved a haunting tale of one such sacrifice and how it brought them the vital gift of corn. Soon after the creation of the world, the legend says, a spirit called Gluskap sat down with another spirit named Nephew in the warmth of the noonday sun. Out of the golden light walked a beautiful maiden who had been born because a drop of dew fell on a leaf and was warmed by the sun, the warming sun of life. "This girl came into being—from the green living plant, from moisture, and from warmth."

Nephew fell in love with the girl and married her. She bore him children, and thus became First Mother. The people multiplied, and gradually their number grew large enough to cause hardship. According to the legend, the people "lived by hunting, and the more people there were, the less game they found. They were hunting it out, and soon starvation came." The hungry children begged First Mother for food, but she had none to feed them. "Be patient," she told them with tears in her eyes. "I will make some food. Then your little bellies will be full." Nephew saw First Mother's distress and asked her what he could do to make her happy again. She answered firmly that he must kill her.

Horrified, Nephew went to Gluskap for advice. But he only repeated what First Mother had said. Then First Mother advised Nephew: "After you have killed me, let two of our sons take hold of my hair and drag my body over that empty patch of earth. Let them drag me back and forth over every part of the patch, until all of my flesh has been torn from my body. Afterward, gather my bones and bury them in the middle of this clearing. Then leave that place. Wait seven moons and then come back, and you will find my flesh there, flesh given out of love, and it will nourish and strengthen you forever and ever." Grief-stricken, Nephew and the children followed her instructions. When seven moons had passed, they

A sweat lodge of the Nez Percé—a squat oval tent of animal hides—sits on a rocky canyon floor in a photograph taken in 1904. A vital part of Indian life, sweat lodges have been used by scores of tribes for physical and spiritual purification. The drawing above shows the willow-branch framework of a typical lodge, whose entrance traditionally faces east and the rising sun. A sacred path leads toward the fire where rocks are heated, then carried into the lodge to produce the steam.

returned to find the land covered with "tall, green, tasseled plants"—corn. The kernels of the corn are First Mother's flesh, "given so that the people might live and flourish."

Similar tales are told of sacrifices that bequeath the nourishment of fish and game to humans. Underpinning all such legends is the conviction that a willing death renews life. The Haida people of the Queen Charlotte Islands off the coast of British Columbia have for generations depended on salmon, much as other tribes have depended on corn—and their legends reflect the same sense of indebtedness to the spirits responsible for offering up the food. One of their stories tells of a boy who lived in a village that was running out of food. The boy's mother offered him the last morsel of salmon, a moldy bit from the bottom of the barrel. The boy took only a small bite and then refused the rest—an incident that met with the disapproval of the Salmon King who resided deep in the ocean. Later, while swimming with friends, the boy was kidnapped by the Salmon People, who named him Salmon Boy and carried him off to their watery home in order to teach him a lesson.

When Salmon Boy grew hungry, the salmon elders gave him permission to catch a salmon child and eat it, but only on one condition—that he must carefully return all of the bones and unconsumed bits of flesh to the river. Salmon Boy did as he was told, but he neglected to return one of the fish's eyes. After finishing his meal, he ran back to join the other children. Among the frolicking youngsters, however, one boy stood apart crying and cupping his eye. The salmon elders asked Salmon Boy if he had followed all their instructions. Sheepishly, he opened his fist to reveal an eyeball, which he quickly threw into the stream. Instantly, the wounded salmon child became whole again.

In the spring of the following year, Salmon Boy swam back to the mainland along with the Salmon People and subsequently was caught by his own mother. Changing back into a boy before her eyes, he became a shaman and devoted himself to healing his people and teaching them the sacred ways. Having come back from death through the grace of the Salmon People, he taught his own people to honor the salmon by committing their bones to the water—an act of reverence that allows the salmon to live again and return intact each spring.

Since all things that pass away will be renewed in time, even the end of the world is an event to be accepted and praised in the legends of Native Americans. According to the Wichitas of the southern Plains, the world began when a voice sang out to the great hunter, Star That Is Al-

An Assiniboin woman performs at a pow-wow held at Lame Deer, Montana, wearing a so-called jingle dress, a garment decorated with dozens of rolled-up snuff can lids. Dresses such as these, which make a rhythmic clinking sound during the dance, are said to have been conceived by an Ojibwa holy man during a vision in the year 1919.

ways Moving, instructing him to shoot the third deer that leaped out of the primordial waters. The first deer was as white as the moon, the second as black as the night sky, and the third a combination of black and white. Star That Is Always Moving shot the black-and-white deer, wounding it with his arrow. And so began the alternation of day and night. The hunter then chased the wounded deer and its two companions into the sky, where they became stars.

In the hope of recapturing his arrow, Star That Is Always Moving has continued to pursue the wounded deer ever since that time. Every year, he gets closer. When at last he finally catches his prey, it is said, the world will come to an end. The sun and the stars will change back into human form, as they were at the beginning, and a new world will commence.

No one has ever expressed this uniquely Indian concept more poignantly than Seattle, chief of the Suquamish tribe, who lived across Puget Sound from the site of the city that later arose in Seattle's name. After his people had signed a treaty ceding most of their tribal land to the United States government in 1854, Seattle addressed the following words in his native tongue to Isaac Stevens, governor of the new Washington territory. Translated into English, his message rings a clear note of renewal, of eternal life, and of hope never ending:

"When the last red man shall have perished, and the memory of my tribe shall have become a myth among the white man, these shores will swarm with the invisible dead of my tribe, and when your children's children think themselves alone in the field, the store, the shop, or in the silence of the pathless woods, they will not be alone. At night, when the streets of your cities and villages are silent and you think them deserted, they will throng with the returning hosts that once filled them and still love this beautiful land. The white man will never be alone. Let him be just and kindly with my people, for the dead are not powerless. Dead, did I say? There is no death, only a change of worlds." ✦

A mask of a killer whale is sometimes worn in a mourning period that precedes winter cere-monies.

FACES OF THE SUPERNATURAL

Ritually attired in strips of cedar bark, ceremonial perform-ers display a range of spirit masks. Be-hind them are a pair of carved poles that define lineage and a special col-umn (center) with holes that a per-former could wrig-gle through during a ritual. The picture was taken in 1915 by Edward Curtis, the great photogra-pher of Indian life.

As the rains of winter envelop the central coast of British Columbia in gloom, strange beings ap-pear in the villages of the Kwakiutl, a people who have lived on these wooded shores for generations. Entering ceremonial houses crowded with onlookers, a multitude of su-pernatural spirits—de-monic birds, ghosts, grizzlies, wolves, and other creatures, the majority of them represented by carved masks—dem-onstrate their ancient potency in dance and dramatic pantomime. For audience and participants alike, these winter rites reaffirm the identity of the Kwakiutl and remind them of the unpredictable forces residing in forest, sky, and sea. It is a time of acknowledgment and appeasement, a time of deepest truths.

Even though the dances executed in the wintertime represent Kwakiutl spirituality at its most dramatic, the peoples' covenant with the supernatural abides from day to day. Wood, especially red cedar, is their prime expressive medium. Shaped in earlier days with sharpened stone or shell and now with steel, wood is transformed into message-laden carved poles, house posts, bowls, rattles, and a variety of other objects in addition to the extraordinary masks used in the winter dances and lesser ceremonies. The carvings spell out kinship, rank, and privilege, but most of all they connect the Kwakiutl to a distant time when the world was ruled by animals endowed with power beyond imagining. In encounters of many kinds, those supernatural creatures conferred some of their power on ancestral humans, the forebears of Kwakiutl hereditary clans. Forever after, it would be the duty of Kwakiutl people to make the ancestral links manifest—most vividly by means of masks that recast humans in the form of a spirit.

THE DIVINELY POSSESSED

Grotesquely tufted with hair, ghost masks figure in the most important winter ceremony, the so-called Hamatsa Dance, performed by a society whose members claim power from a dire spirit known as Cannibal at the North End of the World. During the rites, a person being initiated into the society visits the underworld in the company of ghosts, an episode often heightened by magical effects: Sometimes the initiate will journey to the underworld by falling into a hole prepared in the floor of the ceremonial house. Ghostly voices might issue from below via a hollow tube of kelp.

Ferocity incarnate, this mask combines a pair of raven effigies and, at the top, the visage of a major character in the Hamatsa Dance—a cannibal bird that is said to crave human flesh, feasting on eyeballs and bursting skulls open with its long beak to get at the brains within. Both the cannibal bird and the raven are associates of the ceremony's presiding spirit, Cannibal at the North End of the World, who is too dreadful to be looked upon directly. Like many masks, this composite construction can be manipulated by strings. The three beaks open together, and at the same moment, the jaw of the central face drops down to reveal a sheet of copper.

The Fool Dancer, represented by this huge-nosed mask, serves as a messenger for the initiate in the Hamatsa ceremony and also enforces proper behavior by loudly threatening members of the audience, swinging a club, and even throwing stones. His power is said to be derived from a race of supernatural beings who lived on an inland lake, had enormous, continuously running noses, and hated whatever was serene or clean. Any reference to noses, smell, or mucus during the Hamatsa ritual propels the Fool Dancer into a frenzy.

A wolf mask, fanged and fierce, comes to life in a winter ceremony known as the Dlugwala Dance, which recounts how supernatural power was wrested from this great hunter of the forests. Kwakiutl legend says that the power was stolen by another supernatural creature, Mink, who killed the sons of Wolf and then, donning a disguise, took their place in an initiation ceremony intended to pass on the father's knowledge.

IMAGES OF
THE CLANS

Assembled from wood, copper, and cloth, this wasp mask—like the masks shown on the opposite page—is worn during Kwakiutl ceremonies to represent a clan whose members are linked by heredity. A large number of insects—bee, mosquito, gnat, and midge, in addition to the wasp—play parts in Kwakiutl legends telling of the world's dawn.

This mask of a supernatural being named Kolus, younger brother of the powerful sky spirit known as Thunderbird, is worn on the forehead, above a blanket that conceals the dancer's face. As with all family-crest masks, its use is an inherited privilege, passed down primarily through the female line by marriage.

A sense of darkness and danger is stirred by a dancer masked as an owl, a bird believed to embody the souls of the recently dead. During the performance of the part, the dancer mimics owl behavior, staring at the audience with head thrust forward, crouching immobile for long periods, then moving with great rapidity.

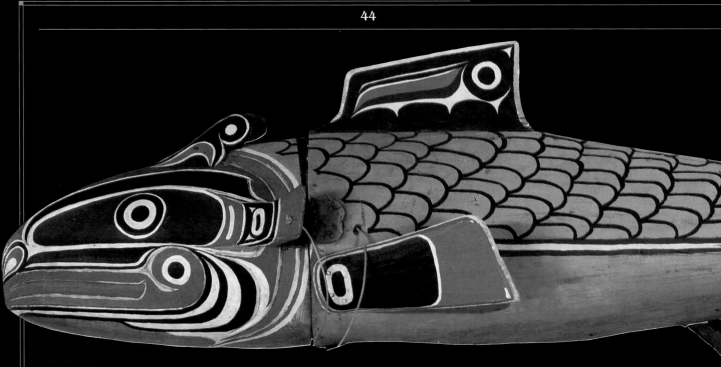

In Kwakiutl myth, supernatural creatures gave shape and order to the world by changing themselves into animals or humans, often bestowing some of their power in the process. Dancers dramatize such connections by the mechanical magic of transformation masks like the one shown in two views here. In its closed state, the mask represents a salmon, crucial to Kwakiutl livelihood along with shellfish, seals, and other marine creatures. When the dancer pulls a string, the head of the salmon abruptly opens to reveal a serpentlike being called a sisiutl. A Kwakiutl legend tells of a man who caught a strange-looking salmon but was unable to kill it until he bit his tongue and spit some blood on the fish. He then saw that he had actually killed a sisiutl, a creature so formidable that it could slay a man with a glance. The fisherman rubbed some of the sisiutl's blood on his infant son, who grew up to be a mighty warrior.

Widemouthed and bearded with cedar bark, this family-crest mask commemorates a sea monster known as Yagim, who wielded great power in the realm that supplied much of the Kwakiutl's livelihood. Legends describe Yagim as a sharklike spirit that trails behind canoes, sometimes capsizing them and devouring the humans as they flail in the waves. In a baleful mood, the monster can whip up raging storms, cause the sea to boil, and destroy whole tribes.

Beneficence and horror are combined in the spirit called Wild
Woman of the Woods, a sleepy-eyed
giantess represented with lips pursed
to utter the chilling cry "Hu! Hu!" She
savors tender human flesh and carries
a basket used to collect small children in
the course of her wanderings in the forest.
But if properly appeased, she is a bringer of
treasure and good fortune—a role celebrated in the first of the sacred ceremonies that
are staged by the Kwakiutl each winter.

2

THE WISDOM OF THE CREATURES

Wearing a deer's head with antlers wrapped in bright pink cloth called sewa (flowers), symbolizing divine grace, a modern Yaqui performs a centuries-old deer-calling dance. Although they no longer rely on deer for meat and clothing, the Yaqui of southern Arizona and northern Mexico continue to perform the dance as part of their rich tribal heritage.

One day a herdsman named Wok Vake'o decided to give up his flocks of sheep and goats and become a hunter, according to a legend told by the Yaqui Indians of the Sonoran Desert in modern-day Arizona. After crafting a bow and many arrows, he set out into the wilderness in search of deer and other prey, hoping to use their hides to make himself some new clothes. While resting early one morning on a tree stump atop a hill, Wok Vake'o caught sight of three deer—two large and one small—by the bank of a river below. The two large deer stood face to face, their heads lowered and their antlers interlocked. As he watched, the pair started to move their heads rhythmically back and forth, scraping their horns together. Thrilled by the sound, the small deer jumped into the air, then ran to its companions and began circling them, leaping about happily. Wok Vake'o did not raise his bow, for he had no desire to kill the beguiling animals. He believed that the big deer were singing and that they were using their antlers as musical instruments to accompany their song. And the small deer, he felt certain, was dancing to the music.

Soon the deer ended their performance and disappeared into the woods. Wok Vake'o walked away, fervently wishing he could sing like the deer. The following morning, he found a fawn deserted by its mother at the foot of another hill. It had been nursed in an enchanted place called the Flower World, home to perfect creatures that serve as the models for their kind. He picked up the fawn and carried it home, composing a song for the deer as he traveled. When he reached his village, he talked with his friends and explained to them that he wanted to sing the deer song. Using two sticks, he showed his friends how to mimic the music of deer antlers. Then he taught a young boy how to dance in the same manner as the small deer he had watched.

Thus do the Yaqui people explain the origin of one of their most ancient and important ceremonies, the Deer Dance. In the stringent Sonoran environment, the deer that haunt the hillsides and riverbanks have long been regarded by the Yaqui not simply as an indispensable source of

In one of the oldest and best-known Pueblo ceremonies, early-20th-century Hopi dancers perform with a swarm of snakes to honor the serpent deities and ensure abundant rainfall. One version of the ritual enacts the legend of a young Hopi man who tried to find the origin of all waters by following the Colorado River to its source. Along the way, the youth was initiated into the Snake Clan by the Great Snake himself, who controlled the waters of the world from his kiva.

food and hide but as creatures possessed of far-reaching powers. For countless generations, people have appealed to the deer spirit to cure illness and infertility, or to summon rain, thunder, and lightning. Before embarking on a hunt, the Yaqui have performed the Deer Dance to appease the spirit guiding the animals and ask its permission to track and kill some of the creatures. Only with the help of the spirit, they believe, could there be a successful hunt.

This show of respect for the spirit of an animal about to be hunted has characterized virtually all Native American cultures. Indeed, the first fur-clad hunters who ventured across the land bridge from Siberia in the depths of the Ice Age to populate the New World may well have felt such reverence for the beasts they preyed on and instilled that attitude in their far-ranging descendants. In time, animals that gave generously of their flesh and bone would be held sacred by Indians in every conceivable setting, from the Inuit hunting seals in the waters of the Arctic, to the Cheyenne pursuing buffalo across the plains, to the Ojibwa tracking beaver and bear in the deep woods of the upper Midwest. Before, during, and after the hunt, people would offer prayers and gifts to the hunted animal's spirit as well as observe elaborate cleansing rituals.

The significance of animals to Native American cultures has extended far beyond hunting ceremonies, however. Apart from their age-old contribution to the material welfare of tribes, many creatures have commanded respect both for their keen instincts and for their uncanny physical gifts, prompting Indians to regard them not as inferior species but as embodiments of higher powers that humans can draw on if they first pay tribute to the spirits that inhabit the beings. For this reason, animal characters have come to play an inspirational role in all aspects of tribal life, from the curing of illnesses to the very structuring of society.

To many Native American peoples, the earth itself was thought to be an animal—a giant turtle floating in a vast, endless sea. Some Indians still refer to North America as "Turtle Island." In California, when earthquakes occur, parents have been heard to tell their children that the Great Turtle has stretched its limbs.

Other animals have loomed large as well in Indian conceptions of the cosmos. The Pawnee people of the Plains, for example, said that the Great Spirit had propped up the heavens by placing a huge buffalo bull in the northwestern corner of the sky—the direction from which great herds of migrating buffalo appeared in the fall. According to the legend, each

SNAKE—FOR STOMACH AND KIDNEY AILMENTS

The Pima and Papago Indians of the Sonoran Desert trace the origin of many ills to wrong behavior toward an array of potentially harmful entities, mostly animals. The curing ritual often involves the use of a carved image of the animal believed to be the cause of the illness. The fetishes, some of which are shown at right, are pressed onto the afflicted areas of the patient's body to help extract the malevolent influences.

year one hair would fall from the giant bull. When all the hairs fell out, the world would come to an end. The Algonquin people of the eastern woodlands believed that the same spirit that animated the great white hare sometimes entered the sun as it raced toward the horizon. Among the Dakota Indians, an owl known as Hin-Han was thought to guard the entrance to the Milky Way, which the souls of the dead were compelled to cross in order to reach the land of the spirits. Any soul that displeased the owl would be tossed into a bottomless abyss.

As old as the earth itself, animals not only helped to create the human race in a number of Indian tales but also served as mentors who taught people the mysteries of the natural world. Over time, it was said, people grew proud and forgot many of those secrets, but their descendants retained the power to salvage the lost wisdom by acknowledging their debt to the animals and heeding their ancient lessons. This type of communication remains possible because the barrier between humans and animals is believed to be slight. Both groups have souls, the legends attest, and animals have been known to transform themselves into human form at will. To the Haida people of British Columbia, for example, the ability of bears to walk upright and use their forepaws as hands signifies their ancient kinship to humans—an affinity that once made it possible for bears to talk and take human mates.

Intermarriages between humans and animals—especially bears—are common in the tales of Indian peoples. Several communities tell the story of the wily Bear Woman, who used her powers to assume a human guise and wed an unsuspecting warrior. The marriage did not last, for the Bear Woman eventually reverted to her animal ways, but

HORNED TOAD—FOR RHEUMATISM AND FOOT SORES

GILA MONSTER—FOR FEVERISH BABIES AS WELL AS BODY SORES

the warrior and other humans similarly drawn into such magical unions acquired knowledge from their animal consorts, which they in turn passed on to future generations. "We know what the animals do, what are the needs of the beaver, the bear, the salmon, and other creatures, because long ago, men married them and acquired this knowledge from their animal wives," explained an Athapaskan hunter of the interior Northwest early in the 20th century. "The white man has been only a short time in this country and knows very little about the animals. We have been here thousands of years and were taught long ago by the animals themselves."

In the beginning, Indian legends affirm, animals and humans spoke the same language. The animals took care of the humans, bringing them fruit, vegetables, and water to drink. During the winter, when food was scarce, they even sacrificed their own flesh so that the humans would survive until spring brought new life to the land. Using their innate ability to predict changes in nature, they would inform the humans of coming storms or seasonal shifts in the weather so that the necessary preparations could be made. In time, however, people began to enslave the animals and abuse them, making the woodpecker drill holes in the trees to gather sap, for example, and setting the beaver to work felling trees for logs. The humans also set animal against animal, ordering an eagle or a hawk to bring them a rabbit for dinner, or commanding a fox to retrieve a partridge. Worse still, humans robbed the animals, snatching their winter stores of food. Eventually, the animals tired of the mistreatment and punished the ungrateful humans by going off to live by themselves and refusing to speak the same language. People were left to fend for themselves.

Despite the rift that developed between animals and humans, the bond between the two groups remained strong in the context of legend and lore—so strong, in fact, that Native American languages do not even have words to distinguish the concepts *human* and *animal*. Early in the 20th century, when an outsider asked the Achumawi people of California what their word was for *animal*, he was told they did not have one. When pressed, they could only offer a phrase meaning "the beings that are world-over, all-living," a description encompassing humans as well as

In a photograph taken in the 1890s, Hupa men carrying obsidian knives (foreground) and displaying the pelts of albino deer perform the White Deerskin Dance, part of the World Renewal ceremony held annually by Indians peoples in northern California. This slow, plaintive dance demonstrated thanks for the blessings of the past and petitioned the powers for good fortune in the future.

animals—and even rocks, which the Achumawi also believed were alive. The Achumawi did have a term for people of European descent, however, a word signifying *tramps*. From the perspective of the Achumawi, the Europeans seemed to be divorced from the natural world and its creatures and thus appeared homeless.

By regarding animals as partners with wisdom to bestow, Indians have gleaned many useful insights. Anthropologist Alfonso Ortiz of New Mexico's Tewa people told of a group of engineers who surveyed a Chippewa reserve in the Canadian Midwest, seeking a place to build an earthen dam. "They thought they'd found a spot," Ortiz wrote, "but a medicine man who was watching their activities told them, 'Not here. The dam won't hold. The earth is not right.' They laughed, but they humored the medicine man and sent a sample of the soil to Ottawa to have it tested.

When the analysis came back, it vindicated the old Chippewa's judgment. The scientists and engineers were mystified as to how this unschooled old man could know something they hadn't even suspected. The Chippewa explained: 'The beaver will not use earth from this area. And if the beaver will not use it, that means it's not good for damming up water.' "

Like their human counterparts, the animals depicted in Indian legends can sometimes be wayward or mischievous. Several creatures—the most notable of which were the coyote, raven, and rabbit—appear as supernatural tricksters, whose antics sometimes turn out to be more foolish than fiendish. In one story, for example, Coyote gets his head stuck in a buffalo skull while trying to watch a ceremony performed by flies; in another, Rabbit becomes so disoriented that his left and right arms end up fighting and injuring each other. When the tricksters are at their boldest and shrewdest, however, they emerge as mythical figures on the order of the fabled Greek hero Prometheus, who was chained to a mountaintop for stealing fire from the gods and passing it to the human race. Various Indian legends celebrate tricksters who risked punishment in the distant past to carry fire to the world's first people. And the Haida Indians tell their version of the widespread myth of the rebellious Raven who carried daylight to humans so that they would no longer have to hunt in darkness.

The Nez Percé people of the Northwest trace their very origins to the heroic exploits of the crafty Coyote. Long before people inhabited the earth, the legend recounts, a monster stalked out of the northern woods and devoured all of the animals—except Coyote. Angered over the loss of his friends, Coyote climbed the tallest mountain, tied himself to its peak with a strong rope, and challenged the monster to eat him. The monster tried to suck Coyote from the mountaintop, but the rope proved to be too strong. Recognizing Coyote's cleverness, the monster befriended him and invited him to come stay with him. Several days into the visit, Coyote asked to go see his friends in the monster's stomach, to which his host agreed. Once inside, Coyote freed the animals by kindling a fire and cutting out the monster's heart.

In order to commemorate his feat, Coyote decided to create a new animal. He flung pieces of the corpse in all directions. Wherever they landed—on the plains, along rivers, in the woods—a tribe of Indians sprang up. When Coyote had finished, his friend the Fox pointed out to

him that he had neglected to create any tribe on the spot where he had killed the monster. Coyote regretted the omission, but he had no more monster parts. Then an idea occurred to him. He wrung the monster's blood from his hands and let the drops fall to the earth. "Here on this ground I make the Nez Percé," he declared. "They will be few in number, but they will be strong and pure."

Another fantastic beast of Indian lore that sometimes comes to the aid of humans is the thunderbird, a giant sky creature said to flash lightning from its beak and eyes and make thunderclaps with its flapping wings. A variety of legends and carvings portray this supernatural being as part animal and part man—with a human face and an eagle's beak, or with an eagle's head and a human face on its abdomen. To the Makah, who live along Washington State's Olympic Peninsula, Thunderbird was once a giant man who changed into a bird in order to hunt whales and other creatures from the sea. One story tells of how Thunderbird

Fashioned by a Clayoquot artist of the Pacific Northwest in the late 19th century, a muslin dance robe bears a colorful image of the mythical thunderbird, an important spirit for many Indian peoples. The two undulating lightning serpents depicted at the lower edge of the robe are often associated with the thunderbird and are usually described as his belt and his harpoon.

snatched a whale out of the sea and delivered it to a Makah village, thereby saving the people from famine. The Sioux call thunderbirds Wakinyan and regard them as stern but fair judges of the people. "The thunder beings are guardians of the truth," explained the Sioux medicine man John Lame Deer. "When you're holding the sacred pipe and you swear on it, you can say nothing but the truth. If you lie, the Wakinyan will kill you with their lightning bolts."

In spite of the fact that thunderbirds can strike terror into the hearts of people, they also defend humans against the sinister water monsters that figure prominently in a great number of Indian legends. One such water monster, known to the Cheyenne as Minio, was said to lie in wait for innocent victims in lakes and streams, and only the great Thunderbird—the leader of the sky creatures—could rescue the people who were snared. John Lame Deer related the story of an epic conflict that took place between the highflying thunderbirds and deadly water monsters the Sioux called Unktehi—serpents that had no use for the human race. "What are these tiny, licelike creatures crawling all over the place?" the Unktehi complained when humans trespassed on their rivers and lakes. "We don't want them around!" To rid themselves of the human pests, the water monsters began to puff themselves up, causing floods that killed many people and alarmed the compassionate thunderbirds. "What's to be done?" the great Thunderbird asked. "I like these humans. They respect us; they pray to us. If they dream of us, they get a little of our power, and that makes them relatives of ours, in a way."

According to the Sioux legend, the thunderbirds decided that if they were going to preserve humanity, they would have to attack the water monsters. A fierce battle was said to have raged back and forth all across the land until, ultimately, the thunderbirds released all of their bolts in a single, terrible blast: "The forests were set on fire, and flames consumed everything except the top of the rock on which the humans had taken refuge. The waters boiled and then dried up. The earth glowed red-hot, and the Unktehi, big and small, burned up and died, leaving only their dried bones in the Mako Sicha, the Badlands, where their bones turned to rock."

A sinister wooden mask with a blood-stained face and toothy grin represents Worm-man, an Inuit conception that combines the features of human and worm, or caterpillar. Like many Inuit spirits, this being was hostile to humans and had to be cajoled into allowing people to live in peace.

For help in meeting the trials inherent in everyday life, Indians have traditionally appealed to the spirits of familiar creatures rather than supernatural ones. According to the lore of numerous tribes, each animal, from the tiny butterfly to the massive buffalo, possesses special powers, or medicines, which can be imparted to humans who understand and respect them. The butterfly, for instance, exemplifies elusiveness. Before setting off into battle, some Indian warriors painted their bodies with butterfly symbols to invoke the insect's power and thus help themselves dodge the arrows and bullets of their enemies. Another creature common to the Indian environment, the turtle, has been associated by many tribes with longevity—a belief that was inspired by the ancient appearance of the animals, by their capacity to retreat into their shells when threatened, and by their mythical association with the primordial earth rising up out of the water. In order to bless a baby with long life, parents would sew the child's umbilical cord into a small stuffed turtle made of deerskin. Each time children touched this talisman, it was said, they would receive some of the turtle spirit's medicine for long life. Turtles could also make humans tougher. Among the Sioux, people who were facing ordeals sometimes fortified themselves by

eating the heart of a turtle. An even more potent source of strength was the bear, whose powers were often invoked before entering battle. Warriors sometimes painted their faces with marks resembling bear claw scratches and carried double-edged knives with handles carved from the jawbones of bears as good-luck charms. It was believed that bear power could also cure illness. Shamans or medicine men from many different groups—including the Sioux, the Chippewa, and the Pueblo peoples—

A wooden parrot from Zuni Pueblo is decorated with colors that represent warmth and the sun itself. The Zuni obtained parrots, whose feathers they prized for use in ceremonies, through trade with other Indian peoples who lived farther south.

frequently dressed as bears when working to heal the sick. Just as honoring the bear spirit could bring blessings to people, provoking the spirit might bring them harm. For that reason, some tribes, most notably the Apache, forbade their hunters to kill a bear, or even to touch the carcass of one found dead in the woods.

Similarly, a number of Indian communities outlawed the killing of eagles, creatures that were revered as lords of the air. This restriction made it extremely difficult for warriors to gather the eagle feathers that could put them in touch with the bird's keen predatory spirit. In a remarkable display of bravery, the Iroquois warrior obtained the coveted feathers by lying down in a large hand-dug trench and covering himself with brush so that he could not be seen from above. Bait was then placed on top of the brush. When an eagle swooped down to snatch the bait, the warrior would attempt the dangerous maneuver of grabbing and holding onto the raptor with one hand while plucking a feather or two with the other. To Native Americans, the eagle embodied not only ferocity but also purity, for it flew high in the atmosphere, where the air was clearest—and where, in the belief of many Indians, the Great Spirit resided. Those who wished to ask something of the Great Spirit sometimes sent their message by way of the eagle spirit.

For the Plains Indians, no creature stood closer to the Great Spirit than the buffalo. Relying as they did on the flesh, skin, and bones of that animal for almost everything they needed—be it food, clothing, shelter, or tools—the people of the Plains addressed prayers directly to the generous buffalo, confident that the animal would serve as their intermediary with the Great Spirit. Those prayers brought many blessings. According to a legend passed down through the generations by the Sioux, the sacred peace pipe was given to their ancestors by White Buffalo Calf Woman, a beautiful maiden who, after teaching the Sioux how to use the pipe, changed herself into a white buffalo calf.

Such a calf was sacrificed by the Kiowa people of the southern Plains in the course of a dance they performed to honor the power of the sun; the various animal parts were then used not only for healing ceremonies but also for worship. A story related by the Kiowa woman Old Lady Horse praises the buffalo herds for coming to the defense of the people when white men constructed a railroad across the tribe's hunting grounds and began to graze cattle there. Incensed, the buffalo uprooted the train tracks with their hoofs, trampled on the white men's gardens, and chased the cattle from the ranges. The white men retaliated with firearms, however, and soon there were only a few buffalo remaining. The surviving animals withdrew into the heart of an enchanted mountain where the rivers ran fresh and the grass was forever green. "Into this world of beauty the buffalo walked," the storyteller concludes, "never to be seen again."

Since time immemorial, many Indians seeking assistance from an animal spirit have decorated their tools and weapons with a fetish, or emblem, of the creature's power. To ensure success on the battlefield and in the hunt, the Crow and Blackfoot peoples covered their arrows with rattlesnake skins to give their weapons the ability to strike with snakelike swiftness. The Inuit engraved their harpoons with images of wolves, which were renowned for their predatory powers. Some seal hunters along the Northwest Coast carried animal fetishes—a raven's beak, perhaps, or a seal's tooth—in pouches worn around their necks or sewn into their clothing, believing that the spirit inhabiting the fetish would communicate with the spirit of their prey and secure its cooperation or deflect its anger. On the Great Plains, hunters sought similar protection or help from the spirits of the animals they tracked by wrapping braided buffalo-hair ropes around their necks.

Among many Indian peoples, particularly those of the Great Plains, the most important fetish was a collection of spiritually charged articles known as a medicine bundle. Still carried by some Indians today, each bundle consists of an array of charms—such as beads, stones, dried herbs, and the claws, teeth, or other parts of animals—wrapped in a pouch made from the skin of the creature with whom the bundle's owner has established a special relationship. Traditionally, the selection of this skin, and of the other objects in the bundle, would be revealed to the owner in a vision or dream. A young man who had a vivid vision of a beaver, for example, would fashion his bundle out of beaver skin. According to the Crow tradition, a warrior who dreamed of the moon had to include an owl skin in his bundle, for the owl was considered the moon's representative; if he dreamed of water, he had to include the skin of an otter, leader of the water animals.

Each medicine bundle imposed special taboos on its owner. The possessor of a beaver bundle, for example, could never show fear of water, the beaver's favorite element. The owner of a snake bundle was forbidden to break animal bones within the home because snakes squeezed and swallowed their prey instead of dismembering them. Some Indian communities had communal bundles, cared for and venerated by all

Mimicking the all-seeing eagle on its perch, dancers from the Rio Grande pueblo of Cochiti in New Mexico begin the ceremony that is held in honor of this sacred bird of prey. The dance is performed throughout the Southwest, where the eagle is regarded as a spiritual messenger whose lofty realm connects the worlds of earth and sky.

members and passed on from generation to generation. The Pawnee, for example, invoked the power of a collective medicine bundle called the "storm eagle"—an eagle hide stuffed with magical objects—whenever they wished to bring down a storm on their enemies.

Many young men—as well as some young women—sought the animal spirit that would become their lifelong helper by going on a vision quest, an ordeal that usually involved fasting and other forms of deprivation. During these quests, the seekers would pray for guidance and instruction from the spirits. Crazy Horse, the great Sioux chief, went on such a quest when he was 12 years old. After witnessing the senseless shooting of the old leader, Conquering Bear, by white soldiers on the Oregon Trail, the young Crazy Horse climbed alone into the hills above the spot where his father and other Sioux men had camped. There, he fasted and kept himself awake for two nights by walking about with sharp stones between his toes. He waited patiently for a vision or message from a spirit, but none came. On the third day, exhausted and delirious, the boy collapsed onto the ground under a large cottonwood tree and fell into a deep sleep. Suddenly, the vision he had longed for appeared to him. He dreamed of a man riding through a violent thunderstorm on a yellow-spotted war-horse. The rider had painted each of his cheeks with a jagged lightning bolt and his body with the marks of hailstones. Above his head flew a small red-backed hawk. As the man rode nearer, a crowd of people

On this Pawnee pipe bowl carved from stone, a bear spirit instructs a shaman about animal wisdom. The Pawnee revered the bear and, by extension, respected members of the elite bear society for their powers as healers and warriors. Other tribes, however, believed that members of the Bear Clan were—like the bear— quick-tempered and even dangerous.

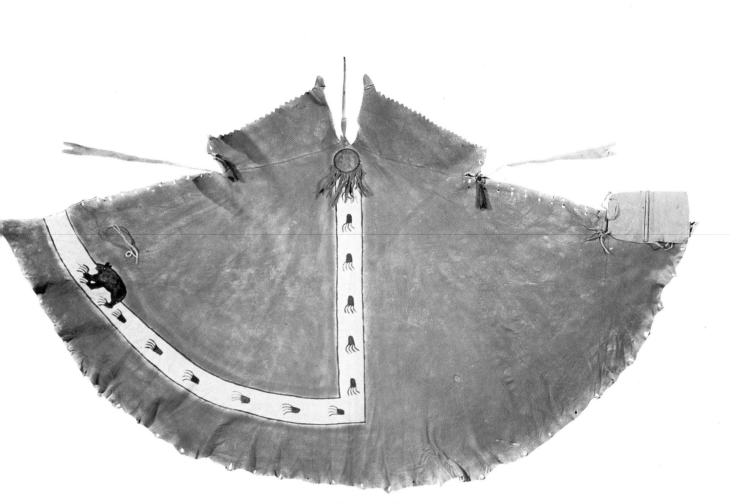

A model of a tipi cover commemorates the vision of a Kiowa warrior of the southern Plains named Bear Bringing It who died in 1849. Painted almost 50 years after his death for the Tennessee Centennial Exhibition, this design of a bear and its paw prints was likely associated with healing the sick.

appeared, reaching out their arms to the rider and creating a great noise. Crazy Horse could sense the rider's mixed feelings of sadness, despair, and pride. Then, abruptly, the dream ended.

Crazy Horse was awakened by his father, who scolded him for going off on his own in such dangerous country. Crazy Horse did not tell his father of his vision until several years later, when he had come to adulthood. His father, a medicine man, told him that the dream had great significance and that the boy should adopt the dream's symbols as his own. Afterward, whenever Crazy Horse went into battle, he painted himself with marks of lightning and hailstones and wore in his hair the skin of a red-backed hawk—the bird he adopted as his personal spiritual helper.

Then as now, Indians who experienced visions of certain animals would sometimes organize themselves into cults, with special rituals and responsibilities. Such cults were dedicated to a variety of animals, including wolves, buffalo, bear, black-tailed deer, mountain sheep, dogs, horses, and rabbits. A vision alone, however, was not enough to guarantee someone membership in a cult. A person would have to display behavior indicating that he or she had received the blessing of a particular spirit.

As a result,
a young man
who dreamed
of salmon
would be required
to show himself over
a period of time to be a
good fisherman. Only
then would the members
of a vision cult invite him
to become a part of their group.
The Elk Dreamers, an important
vision cult among the Sioux, possessed power over matters of love.
Similar to other Indian peoples, the
Sioux were impressed by the bull elk's
ability to call and attract females, and they
regarded the elk spirit as a great helper in find-
ing someone to love. Any man who became an
Elk Dreamer, they believed, was sure to marry before
long. During the performance of their dances, the Elk
Dreamers wore triangular masks made of animal skins with branches attached to resemble antlers. They carried small hoops with mirrors at the
center and believed that they could win the heart of a young woman by
catching sunlight in the mirror and throwing it into her eyes as she
watched the dance. Some tribes had female elk cults that performed their
own elaborate dance once a year. In most tribes, women could form other vision cults as well. Sioux women, for example, had counterparts to
almost all of the male societies except the bear cult. Sioux tradition held
that women never dreamed of bears.

In addition to the vision cults, many Indian peoples developed animal
clans, or societies, some of which remain active today and cut across
tribal lines. Typically, a community would contain several of these clans,
with the membership of each drawn from both sexes. The Mohawk of the
northeastern woodlands, for example, developed three animal clans—
Wolf, Bear, and Turtle. Since the Mohawk, like other tribes belonging to
the Iroquois league, were matrilineal, newborn children joined the clan of
their mother, but in patrilineal societies children would inherit their father's affiliation. Among some peoples, when an outsider from another

*A grizzly bear mask dating from the ear-
ly 19th century was worn by the Tlingit
people of southeast-
ern Alaska to em-
body the spirit of
the beast. The real-
istic carving consists
of wood covered
with the skin of a
bear's head, iron
balls for eyes, cop-
per lips, teeth of
snail shell, and
bear's canines.*

tribe or from the white world joined the community, an elder woman would adopt the newcomer, who then became a member of her clan. After Europeans settled in North America, the Ojibwa created two new clans for children of their tribe who had English or American fathers; these were the Lion and the Bald Eagle, so titled for the animal symbols associated with the two nationalities.

A clan might contain many unrelated families, although all of its members were considered relatives of the clan's guiding spirit, or totem—a word derived from the Ojibwa term *odem,* signifying the mystic bond between the spirit, the place, and the people. As a consequence of this common ancestry, members of the same clan were forbidden to intermarry, even if they came from different tribes. Even today, parents who see their children becoming attracted to a clan "sister" or "brother" may take steps to discourage the relationship.

Over the generations, clans have preserved legends that explain their origins. Such tales often concern a lost hunter or curious youth who finds himself in an unfamiliar and dangerous place, where he receives help and

Dressed in the skin and mask of a bear, a Sioux shaman leads hunters in a bear dance in this 1835 painting by George Catlin. The Sioux, who were very fond of bear meat and required great quantities of bear grease to oil their hair and bodies, believed that by imitating the movements and sounds of their prey in dance, they could convince the bear to sacrifice itself later in the hunt.

Their faces blackened, two buffalo dancers at Nambe Pueblo in New Mexico hold traditional gourd rattles and bows and arrows in preparation for the dance. Although buffalo are now scarce in the Southwest, many communities continue to honor the animals upon whom their ancestors depended.

guidance from an animal. The wanderer then returns to his village and sets up a clan to honor the animal and teach its secrets to other people. In an Osage legend, a seeker ventured into the wilderness to find an animal that would show itself to him and become his totem. Foolishly, he tracked only the deer—a creature he thought would be a worthy symbol of his clan—and ignored signs of all the other animals around him. One day, with his eyes focused downward on the deer tracks, he stumbled into a large spider web and fell to the ground. Rising up, he struck angrily at the spider, which scurried out of reach. The spider asked its tormentor why he was blundering through the woods as if blind, staring at the ground. The man explained that he was seeking a totem for his clan. "I could be such a symbol," the spider ventured, pointing out that while it might appear small and weak, it possessed the great virtue of patience. "All things come to me," the spider said proudly. "If your people learn this, they will be strong indeed." Recognizing the wisdom in those words, the man returned to his village and made the spider the totem of his clan.

The Osage Spider Clan was typical of Native American communities in that it was headed by a man. But within the clans of the Iroquois and other matrilineal peoples, women served as the leaders. Each Iroquois clan had an elder woman, or Clan Mother, as its head. Together, the Clan Mothers possessed important responsibilities within the community as a whole, including choosing the men who would serve as Iroquois chiefs. If a chief failed to perform his duties in the manner expected, the Clan Mothers would give him a warning. After issuing three warnings, they took away his chieftaincy.

People frequently attributed the characteristics of a clan's totem to its members. Accordingly, those who belonged to the Bear Clan were described as strong and sometimes dangerous, while members of the Turtle Clan were believed to be reserved and methodical in their thinking. Among the Cheyenne, those who joined the clan called the Mouse People were thought to be very attentive to things in their immediate vicinity but blind to the long view.

Whether or not members of a tribe belonged to an animal clan, they often forged special relationships with animal spirits that determined their role

A quartzite buffalo effigy found in Alberta, Canada, figured in the hunting rituals of the northern Plains people some 500 years ago. The statue's stubby legs probably enabled it to stand securely on the irregular surface of an earthen altar.

In this 1832 painting of a Mandan buffalo-calling dance by George Catlin, eight performers wearing willow boughs and buffalo hides mimic the animal's movements in an attempt to lure the herd. The two dancers painted black with white dots represent the "firmament or night," while the dancers painted red with white streaks were "ghosts that the morning rays were chasing away."

in society. A Cheyenne woman named Mary Standing Soldier, who won renown among her people for healing warriors felled in battles with the U.S. Cavalry during the late 19th century, carried with her the claws of a ferocious bear that she was said to have fought off single-handedly as a girl. When serving as a healer on the battlefield, she reputedly would growl like a bear as she removed arrows or bullets from wounded men, lending them the strength they needed to rise up. A descendant who knew her when she was quite old said that she had come to resemble the animal whose power she invoked, with dark hair all over her body.

So close was the bond between humans and animals that many Native American legends told of creatures who formed clans of their own in hidden camps or villages, where they returned to live after they died of natural causes or were killed. Within these villages, the animals removed their fur and feathers and looked and acted like humans. In time, their souls might choose to take animal form again. Since the animals never really died, their spirits had to be treated with the utmost respect so that they would one day return to provide food, clothing, and other essentials for humans. "The greatest peril of life lies in the fact that human food consists entirely of souls," explained an Iglulik hunter of the Far North in the 1920s. "All the creatures that we have to kill and eat, all those that we have to strike down and destroy to make clothes for ourselves, have souls, souls that do not perish with the body." The spiritual duty of the hunter, he added, was to appease those souls, "lest they should revenge themselves on us for taking away their bodies."

Like humans, each of the animal species had its own chief, frequently referred to in legends as the Owner. This ruling spirit, which sometimes took the form of a creature that was larger than others of its kind or differently marked, determined how many of the animals under its charge could be killed by humans. On occasion, it might allow itself to be taken by humans, who were then obliged to pay the spirit homage before they feasted on its flesh. Other animal leaders, or Owners, might assume human form. Pueblo Indians honored one of their own as the Mother of Game and thanked her for leading deer, buffalo, rabbits, and mountain goats to worthy hunters.

Another, far more menacing woman presided over the sea creatures that were hunted by the Inuit who resided in the frigid Arctic. Many of the tribes called her Sedna, or The Great Food Dish, although she was known by other names as well, including Takanaluk, or The Terrible One Down

A scratching tool made from three seal claws lashed to a shaft of wood mimics a seal flipper in appearance. Inuit seal hunters raked such scratchers across the ice, producing the sound of a seal working at its blowhole, in order to lull their suspicious prey. By employing tools that both looked and sounded seal-like, hunters hoped to propitiate the spirits of their quarry.

Under. According to one legend, Sedna was the daughter of two giants. At a young age, she developed an uncontrollable appetite for flesh, seizing it wherever she found it. One night, her parents awoke in agony to find her devouring their flesh. They put her in an umiak—an open hide-covered boat propelled with broad paddles—and took her out to the deepest part of the sea. There, they pushed her overboard, but Sedna clung to the side of the boat, forcing her relentless parents to cut off the joints of her fingers, one by one. As the pieces fell into the water, they were transformed into seals, walruses, whales, and shoals of fish.

Abandoned in the deep, Sedna persevered and became a force to be reckoned with. The Inuit credited her with controlling all activity in or above the water, from the spawning of storms to the annual migration of her offspring, the fish and sea mammals. Whenever famine struck the Inuit, they blamed it on Sedna, saying that she had become angry at them for some reason and had locked away the animals. To pacify her, an Inuit shaman would go into a trance and send his soul flying across the sea to the great whirlpool that marked the entrance to Sedna's home. Once there, he would soothe Sedna by combing her long hair—an act she was not able to perform herself because of the loss of her fingers. Eventually, Sedna would either promise the shaman to release more animals to be hunted or advise him to move his people to another place to find the animals. The soul of the shaman would then journey back to his body. He would sing a song describing what Sedna had told him, and the people would do as she requested.

Sedna and the other animal Owners bestowed their favors only on those hunters who had faithfully observed the required taboos and rituals. To break the taboos meant offending the spirits. As an Inuit hunter once explained when asked why polar bears had failed to appear during that year's hunting season: "No bears have come because there is no ice, and there is no ice because there is too much wind, and there is too much wind because we mortals have offended the powers."

In many communities, the appeasing of the powers began prior to the hunt with an animal-calling ceremony. At the beginning of buffalo hunting season, for example, Plains Indians endeavored to lure buffalo to their camps by singing songs and displaying fetishes such as rare riverbed stones shaped like buffalo heads, or the hard fur balls that buffalo regurgitated after cleaning themselves with their tongues. One Plains tribe, the Mandan, presented bowls of food to a buffalo head, hoping that through this symbolic act of generosity they might entice the buffalo to come.

The Mandan and other tribes of the Plains also staged lengthy and exhausting buffalo-calling dances. Most were performed by men, but when the buffalo were especially scarce, Mandan hunters asked members of the White Buffalo Cow Women cult to dance as well. Artist George Catlin evoked the scene at a buffalo-calling dance he witnessed in a Mandan village along the upper Missouri River in 1832. "The chief issues his order to his runners or criers, who proclaim it through the village—and in a few minutes the dance begins," Catlin recollected. "About 10 or 15 Mandans at a time join in the dance, each one with the skin of the buffalo's head (or mask) with the horns on, placed over his head, and in his hand his favorite bow or lance." The ritual never failed, Catlin added, because the dancers persisted until the buffalo appeared: "Lookers-on stand ready with masks on their heads, and weapons in hand, to take the place of each one as he becomes fatigued and jumps out of the ring. During this time of general excitement, spies or 'lookers' are kept on the hills in the neighborhood of the village, who, when they discover buffalo in sight, give the appropriate signal, by 'throwing their robes,' which is instantly seen in the village and understood by the whole tribe. At this joyful intelligence, there is a shout of thanks to the Great Spirit."

In some Indian communities, dancers would act out the arrival of the animals. Anthropologist Ruth Underhill described a Pueblo deer-calling ceremony she observed in the 1940s at which costumed men played the part of the prey—a ritual that is still performed at a number of Pueblos today. "It was almost dawn when we heard the hunter's call from the hill-

A 19th-century hunter from Kodiak Island, Alaska, wore this realistic decoy helmet while peering from behind a rock or block of ice. The likeness lured the seal to its death while honoring the spirit of the beast.

side," Underhill wrote. "Then shadowy forms came bounding down through the piñon trees. At first we could barely see the shaking horns and dappled hides. Then the sun's rays picked out men on all fours, with deerskins over their backs and painted staves in their hands to simulate forelegs. They leaped and gamboled before the people while around them pranced little boys who seemed actually to have the spirit of fawns." The sprightly Deer Dancers were escorted by their Owner, the Mother of Game, a beautiful woman with long black hair: "She led the animals where they would be good targets for the hunters, and, one by one, they were symbolically killed."

Persuading the prey to offer themselves up was just the first step in the complex spiritual process of obtaining flesh to eat. Many tribes imposed taboos on both hunters and their kin before, during, and after the chase. In order to purify themselves for a whale hunt, for example, Makah men fasted, flogged themselves with stinging nettles, and bathed in secret pools of sacred water. While the hunters were away, their wives lay motionless in their long houses to help ensure that the whale, too, would be submissive. Chippewa hunters fasted before hunts, then blackened their faces with charcoal to show they had properly observed this taboo. Their wives and children were expected to fast and mark themselves in the same fashion while the hunters were away. Hopi women—and those men who were left behind in the village—brought good fortune to their hunters by taking ash from the fires used to cook the prehunt meals and rubbing it behind their ears. They also refrained from evil thoughts while the hunters were gone.

Many communities required men to practice celibacy before a hunt, in the belief that the process of generating life must be separated from the act of taking life if the community was to prosper. For the same reason, menstruating women were often forbidden to touch either the weapons or the food belonging to the hunters. To cleanse their bows and arrows of an accidental contamination of this kind, Papago hunters sang a special song as soon as they left their villages. The Hopi observed a similar custom. To rid themselves of the odor of women and babies, which they thought would alarm antelope and deer, Hopi hunters performed a cleansing ceremony when they arrived at their first campsite. While sitting before a fire, they would sweep their hands over their legs, then bring them to their mouths and blow on them. The movement would be repeated for each part of the body, until the hunter was entirely purified.

The hunt itself was often a highly ritualized affair. When hunters from the Omaha tribe of Nebraska sighted a buffalo herd, they made three ceremonial stops before attacking the animals. Legend says that an impatient hunter, worried that the buffalo might escape, once persuaded a hunting party to forgo the required three stops—and was trampled to death by buffalo the next day. Among many hunting parties, it was customary to speak or sing words of respect to an animal, either right before or after killing it. A hunter made this gesture to let the animal know that he was taking its life as a result of need rather than greed. The hunter might also plead with the animal to put aside anger—not out of fear for his own safety but because he worried that the spirit of the animal and others like it would retreat and provide no more food for his people. When Algonquin hunters of eastern Canada discovered a bear in its den, for example, they would not violate its sanctuary. Instead, they addressed the animal respectfully as "grandfather" and requested that it emerge from its den and

Coast Salish people of the Tulalip Reservation, located in Marysville in the state of Washington, carry the first salmon of the new fishing season reverently on a fern-covered bier (left). Afterward, the community gathered (below) in a ceremony to eat the fish and sing its praises, and to bless the fishermen (with backs to camera) who will be responsible for the season's catch.

allow itself to be killed. If the animal failed to appear after being called three times, the hunters spoke to the animal once again in polite terms, this time calling it "grandmother." In a similar fashion, hunters from southwestern tribes always apologized to a wounded deer before they killed it.

Hunters frequently were required to show respect after the killing of an animal as well. When the Northern Saulteaux, an Ojibwa people, killed a black bear, they dressed it in human clothes as a sign of honor. "If this were not done," explained one Saulteaux, "the spirit of the bear would be offended and would report the circumstances to the chief of bears, who would prevent the careless Indians from catching more." During the course of butchering the bear, a piece of its heart was set aside to be offered later in gratitude to the spirit who had so generously permitted the animal to be killed.

An ivory and wood model commemorates the Inuit Bladder Festival held in the kashim, or social house, every winter during the month of December. Hunters inflated the bladders of the seals killed during the year and entertained them as honored guests at the festival. At the end of the ceremony, the men returned the bladders, which were believed to contain the animals' souls, to the sea. Shown hanging from the roof in the miniature are two wooden bladders, in addition to an ivory carving of a bird.

After successfully harpooning a whale and towing it back to their village, the Inuit of Alaska held a special welcoming ritual for the animal. Wearing ceremonial clothes and facial paint, the wife of the *umelik,* or leader of the hunt, greeted the whale and gave it a drink of fresh water to quench the thirst of its soul, for the Inuit believed that the spirits of all sea creatures loved the taste of fresh water. As she poured the water into the whale's blowhole, the umelik's wife said, "Here is water. You will want to drink. Next spring come back to our boat." Then the other wives of the hunters thanked the whale for permitting itself to be taken from the sea.

Another northern people, the Iglulik, forbade their hunters to perform ordinary activities for three days after killing a bearded seal, polar bear, or whale. Women could not do any sewing until the animal was completely cut up, for fear that the thread would draw evil spirits into the village. A harpoon used to kill a seal had to be placed next to a lighted lamp during the first night after the animal's death because the soul of the seal was thought to reside in the weapon and needed to be kept warm. A man who killed a caribou was required to place a small piece of meat or suet under a stone as an offering to its spirit. He and his family also had to dispose of caribou bones carefully, for to let a dog chew on the bone would show disrespect for the caribou spirits and might cause the animals to vanish.

Most Native American communities held a special ceremony for the first animal killed during a hunting season to ensure that its soul would not speak disparagingly of the hunters when it returned to its animal village and thus discourage the rest of the animal spirits from coming. The Kwakiutl of the Northwest Coast, for example, welcomed the first bear killed each spring into their village with a ceremonial meal. Photographer Edward Curtis, who visited the Kwakiutl in the early 20th century, observed that the hunter who claimed the first kill would carry the bear carcass to the village and call out, "I have a visitor!" All of the villagers would promptly assemble at his house. There, Curtis added, "the bear was placed in a sitting posture in the place of honor at the middle of the back part of the room, with a ring of cedar bark about its neck and eagle down on its head. Food was then given to each person, and a portion was placed before the bear. Great solemnity prevailed. The bear was treated as an honored guest and was so addressed in the speeches. The people, one by one, would advance and take its paws in their hands as if uttering a supplication. After the ceremonial meal was over, the bear was skinned and prepared for food."

Other peoples held similar "first food" ceremonies. When the Tsimshian people of the Northwest caught their first salmon, for example, they immediately notified several of their oldest shamans, who went down to the river to greet the salmon. While one shaman donned fisherman's clothing, the others spread a cedar-bark mat on the ground and placed the salmon on it. Taking up the mat by its corners, the shamans carried the salmon to the village chief's house. The fisherman-shaman led the procession, shaking a rattle in his right hand and waving an eagle's tail in his left. Only selected members of the village were permitted to enter the chief's house and attend the remainder of the ceremony. Inside, the shamans placed the salmon on a cedar board and walked around it four times. When it came time to clean the fish for the ceremonial meal, the shamans used a mussel-shell knife; to cut with a stone or metal knife could bring on a violent thunderstorm. They cut the salmon's head first, then the tail, addressing the fish in honorary terms as they did so.

Some groups also staged lavish ceremonies to mark the conclusion of the hunting season. The Inupiaq of Alaska have for generations conducted a four-day Bladder Festival in early December in order to entertain and please the *inuas,* or souls, of the animals that were killed during the preceding year. Inupiaq tradition stated that an animal's soul resided in its bladder, so the people would carefully collect and store the bladders of all the animals they killed until their souls could be properly honored at the annual ceremony. To prepare for the festival, the Inupiaq cleaned the village kashim, a large ceremonial snowhouse with a central firepit. They inflated the animal bladders, painted them with colorful designs, and hung them from the kashim's walls and ceiling. Amid the bladders, they draped large puppetlike animal effigies whose eyes, heads, wings, and mouths rolled, bobbed, flapped, and opened at the yank of a cord. Dried bundles of wild celery also dangled from the ceiling, to be burned later during the festival's purification rites. A fire was kept constantly ablaze in the pit throughout the festival, and the celebrants were forbidden to make sudden loud noises or unexpected movements for fear of frightening the souls contained in the bladders.

Punctuated by rhythmic songs and dances mimicking the calls and movements of birds and sea mammals, the festival included a symbolic removal of the points from harpoons and hunting darts to pacify the animal inuas, comic speeches to amuse them, and offerings of food to please their *tunghat,* or Owners. On the final night of the festival, the village shaman climbed atop the roof of the kashim and delivered his own speech. Then the hunters gathered up the bladders and followed the shaman, who carried a huge torch of burning wild celery stalks, down to the sea, where a special hole had been chipped in the ice. The hunters marched around the hole and took turns ripping open the bladders and thrusting them under the water. Each man watched and listened carefully to the movements and sounds the bladders made as they sank into the water, hoping to receive a sign from the departing inuas that next year's hunting season would be a success.

At the conclusion of one such Bladder Festival, the shaman went so far as to have himself lowered into the frigid waters so that he could talk directly with the souls before they departed. A few of the submerged souls expressed dissatisfaction with their treatment, he reported afterward, but the rest responded in a way that augured well for the future, assuring him that they were "pleased with the men who had taken them and given them such a fine festival." ✦

WINGED ENVOYS TO THE GODS

Light reflected from its eyes of copper gives an appearance of ferocity to this talisman made from a golden eagle, which a Plains warrior carried in his medicine bundle among his most sacred possessions.

Birds have long been revered by tribal cultures as holy envoys that carry prayers and supplications to the sky spirits and return with blessings of power and guidance to enrich the Indians' earthly existence. Some believe birds to be symbols of the soul, as well as intermediaries to the gods. Seeking their cooperation, Native Americans have plied bird spirits with offerings and performed dances to honor and beseech them. Pleas are sent skyward in the smoke of burning tobacco. Avian objects pervade tribal life; bird images are worn as personal adornment or as talismans during worship; in the past, they were carried into battle to safeguard the bearer. Feathers are often considered the most potent part of the bird, but beaks, bones, talons, and even entire bodies of some birds also have been used to re-create bird spirits. Many such objects have been passed down as cherished symbols of the power bestowed by those creatures that soar in the lofty realms where many of the gods dwell.

This Crow Indian bustle, which dates from the 19th century, is bedecked with valuable bald eagle feathers that dangle nearly to the ground. It was worn by a man during ceremonial dances.

HONORING THE EAGLE

More than any other bird, the eagle has symbolized sacred power to Indian peoples throughout North America. Because the eagle flies so high that it disappears behind the clouds, it has been associated with those spirits residing in the farthest reaches of the heavens that are in control of the elemental forces of nature: rain and wind, thunder and lightning. In addition, the magnificent creature is held in high esteem for its physical attributes; warriors belonging to the Plains tribes wore eagle feathers when they went into battle in the hope of being blessed with eaglelike endurance, quickness, ferocity, and sharpness of eye. In previous times, the hunting of eagles was thought to be a spiritual endeavor, and in some Indian communities, only the most prestigious men were given permission to participate in the hunt.

The design of this Crow bonnet probably conforms to a dream vision experienced by its maker. The golden eagle's head, along with wing and tail feathers, is mounted on a skullcap fashioned of buffalo hide and decorated along the edge with small brass bells.

Feather fans are used today to evoke the eagle's supernatural curative power, just as they were when a Kickapoo Indian made this peyote fan (left) more than 100 years ago. Bald eagle feathers like these were so highly prized that a perfect tail of 12 could fetch its owner a horse in trade.

The Pomo ear ornaments below, carved from willow sticks, feature shell beads, bone, and feathers that depict the head of a woodpecker. The ornaments, eight inches in length, were worn during ceremonial dances.

The striking Yurok Jump Dance headdress below combines woodpecker scalps and bluebird feathers on albino deerskin. The rarity of the components and the intricate workmanship were intended to convince the Supreme Being of the maker's industry and piety.

CRIMSON TREASURE

Many Indian peoples of the American West Coast considered the woodpecker, with its brilliant crimson head, to be a sacred bird that manifested persistence and symbolized the life-sustaining sun. The bird contributed its brightly hued head feathers to intricate and stunning designs that were employed on an array of ceremonial objects.

Because woodpecker scalps were difficult to obtain in large numbers, they were treasured by Native Americans, and their abundant use and display were an indication of wealth and tribal status. So coveted were woodpecker scalps that among some tribes they became a medium of exchange. At funerals, the bereaved demonstrated the depth of their grief by sacrificing to the pyre their baskets decorated with the precious scarlet feathers.

Ceremonial feather belts were highly prized and used as important trade items. The Maidu belt (above) is decorated with quail topknots and acorn woodpecker scalps. A similar belt, made in 1899, bore 228 scalps.

Highlighted by swan feathers and beads, this Maidu plume was worn across the back of the head to denote tribal rank. It contains the scalps of 16 pileated woodpeckers, a significant multiple of four—the Maidu's sacred number.

The pair of sealskin gauntlet gloves shown above was made to be worn by Inuit men during ceremonial dances. Decorating the gauntlets are beaks of horned puffins and long quills of bird feathers that rattled rhythmically to the cadence of a drum beat.

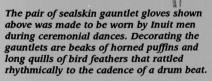

APPEASING AVIAN SPIRITS

For the Inuit, the annual arrival of migratory waterfowl from the south announced the beginning of spring and an end to the hardships of winter. In addition to that happy occurrence, however, the Indians eagerly awaited the bounty that the birds provided: meat and eggs to eat, skins to sew into parkas, bright feathers, down, and beaks to decorate ceremonial masks and costumes as well as baskets, tools, and other utilitarian objects.

In exchange for such gifts, the Inuit honored and appeased the souls of the dead birds with effigies exquisitely carved from wood. Furthermore, they carried parts of birds, a beak or a claw, for example, as charms whose associated spirits might provide help on the hunt or elsewhere.

This amulet, the entire body of a bird wrapped in caribou skin, was in all probability hung on a boat or a sled.

Charms fashioned from the heads and feathers of loons (below) are worn by Inuit women after a successful fishing or hunting expedition at the edge of the coastal ice.

This dance baton features a woodpecker affixed to the shaft with a piece of springlike whale cartilage. Used by a skillful dancer, the bird bobbed, as if pecking the baton, imitating its real-life counterpart.

3

THE POWER IN THE GREEN STALK

Using tobacco to communicate with the spirit world, two Crow Indians smoke long ceremonial pipes. Such pipes were regarded as supernatural beings. "The stone is our blood," wrote one Indian of the prized red catlinite from which many of the finest pipes, including the example above, were carved.

An elder of the Ojibwa community enters the social hall of a Canadian church in the mid-1970s, accompanied by a small retinue of assistants. The group has been on the road all afternoon. Their purpose: to conduct the pipe ritual. As the travelers enter the room, they discover several dozen Native Americans from different tribes—Ojibwa, Ottawa, Mohawk, Cree, and others—assembled there along with a few non-Indians who have been invited to take part.

The crowd parts as the elder and his entourage move toward the west wall of the hall. They instruct the people present to sit in a ring, asking any menstruating women present to sit outside the circle and any who have taken alcohol within the past four days not to smoke the pipe that one of the assistants now removes from the leather bag. The pipe has two parts, a stem of unadorned wood and a stone bowl.

The ceremony begins. As a rite of purification, a second helper ignites a braid of prairie sweet grass, which produces an aromatic smoke pleasing to the spirits. The assistant carries the smoldering twist around the circle, allowing the smoke to pass over each person in the group, then over the pieces of the pipe. He then fits stem to bowl and reverently hands the pipe to the leader, who begins to fill the bowl with tobacco.

As he does so, praying over each pinch and passing it through the sweet grass smoke, he explains the ritual to the congregation, some of whom have never participated in a pipe-smoking ceremony. Tobacco, as well as the sacred pipe in which we smoke it, he says, were among the first gifts of the spirits to the people. We make offerings of tobacco in order to renew the relationship between men and the spirits. We burn it in this sacred pipe knowing that the smoke will carry our words and thoughts to the spirits.

The leader voices a holy song and lights the tobacco. Next, he offers smoke to the spirits by pointing the stem east, south, west, and north, skyward and earthward, and then an assistant carries the pipe clockwise around the circle, pausing at each celebrant. Some take the pipe and perform a brief ritual, perhaps extending it toward the sky and then toward the earth before smoking it or turning it in a circle afterward. Others waft pipe smoke above their heads before solemnly passing the pipe to the person on their left. When the pipe returns to the leader, he sings again, reverently disassembles the instrument, and restores it to the leather bag to conclude the ceremony.

The tobacco smoked that evening is merely one fruit of the earth with which Indians have long felt a supernatural connection. Roots and nuts that they gathered, trees that they felled, crops that they planted, and herbs that they collected for healing were considered gifts from the spirits. As such, they were treated with reverence in daily life. "We do not like to harm the trees," said a Fox Indian of the early 20th century. "Whenever we can, we always make an offering before we cut them down. If we did not think of their feelings, all the other trees in the forest would weep, and that would make our hearts sad, too." Before digging a root or plucking a berry, an Indian would offer an apology or a prayer, then take care not to pick more than would be eaten.

Early Native Americans also developed ceremonies to demonstrate their appreciation for the harvest, every year celebrating the first of each food to ripen. Today the Iroquois of upstate New York, in a ceremony that binds them to these ancient practices, hold an annual festival to commemorate the ripening of the wild strawberry, the earliest fruit of the year. By causing the fruit to ripen, the Iroquois believe, the Creator renews his promise of generosity to the people.

As agriculture took hold, Indians who were living in permanent settlements near their fields developed elaborate rites to praise the earth's bounty and to renew the bond between human beings and the spirits. Ceremonies, which sometimes lasted for many days, required purification by fasting or other dietary restrictions. Celebrants performed songs and dances in propitiation of the spirits. The powers had graciously caused the crops to ripen, and now the Indians wished to provide something for the spirits in return. By adhering strictly to such rites, Indians believed, they would keep harmony with the natural world. The sun would shine, the rains would fall, and the seed would sprout and thrive.

Of all the plants known to ancient Indians, tobacco was among the most sacred. The broad leaves might be offered whole to the spirit of a plant that was to be harvested. Dried to a dull green, they were crumbled and strewn in holy places as an offering to spirits residing there. Sprinkled

Brightly colored cloths representing prayers flutter from the branches of a tree in South Dakota's Bear Butte State Park, an area sacred to the Sioux, Cheyenne, and other Plains Indians who regard it as the center of their universe. The prayers are encouraged heavenward by offerings of tobacco—still packaged in commercial wrappers—at the foot of the tree (right).

onto an open fire in sacrifice to the spirits—as was the custom among the Iroquois, for example—or smoked in pipes and cigars with wrappers of reed or cornhusk, tobacco offered a means of communicating with the spirit world. More potent than the varieties cultivated commercially nowadays, the Indian leaf produced a narcotic effect that was both soothing and stimulating. An outsider who once sampled it marveled at its strength: "Why, four puffs of that would knock you over," he said, referring to the practice of smoking to the four horizons, as well as heavenward and earthward. "I wonder how they ever managed six." The pungent wisps that spiraled upward, Indians believed, carried human thoughts and words into the realm of the supernatural. "The smoke shall rise, and one shall speak," said the Iroquois.

Few Native American customs were more widespread than the ritual use of tobacco. Except for the tribes of the Northwest Coast, every Indian community south of the subarctic offered tobacco to the spirits, not only during special ceremonies but also as part of the rituals accompanying most endeavors. No hunting or raiding party set forth without an appeal to the spirits for success, no crop was planted or harvested, no ailment cured or lover wooed. And in each case, tobacco played a role.

Long before Europeans set foot in North America, the plant had spread northward from its origins in South America through Mexico and the American desert all the way to the latitude of the Hudson Bay and eastward across plains and mountains to the Atlantic Ocean. Some Indian communities traded for the plant; others grew it. But however they got it, Native Americans had diverse beliefs about the origin of this magical plant. Woodland tribes of the Great Lakes region, for instance, saw tobacco as a trust from the Great Spirit. Along with sacred pipes for smoking it, the plant was bestowed on human beings to give them something of value to offer to the powers—the sun, moon, thunder, and water as well as the Great Spirit himself.

Legends of other tribes seem to suggest that this bounty came indirectly from the supernatural. One intriguing account, still told among the Yuchi of Georgia, links tobacco to the seed of man. According to this story, a young couple traveling together left the path to make love. Nine months later, they had a baby boy. "I have a twin brother," announced the child one day. He guided his incredulous father to the place where he had been conceived. There, the older man saw an unfamiliar plant with sweet-smelling yellow flowers. The boy explained that the plant was sacred, a gift from the supernatural, and that its leaves should be dried and smoked. The fumes, he said, would send an offering to the spirits.

The origin of the pipe was as sacred as that of the sacramental leaf that smoldered in the bowl. Sioux legend recounts how White Buffalo Calf Woman brought the pipe to the tribes. Many lifetimes ago, according to the tale, two young hunters looked out from the hilltop where they stood seeking game and saw approaching a beautiful woman in a white buffalo-skin dress. Not only was her apparel a sign of the supernatural, but as the woman neared, the hunters could see that she walked with the slow, stately gait of the spirits and carried a holy bundle on her back. Despite strong taboos protecting spirits from worldly lust, the older man was overcome by desire. As he reached out to touch the woman, a large cloud suddenly covered both of them. When it lifted, the man with impure intentions had become a pile of bones.

Following this demonstration of her powers, the woman sent the remaining hunter home with an order that the chief prepare a large tipi for her. The man did as commanded, and at sunrise the next day, the woman arrived, carrying her bundle in her hands. Unwrapping it, she withdrew the stem of a pipe with her right hand, the bowl with her left. (To this day, the Sioux carry their sacred pipes in this manner.) White Buffalo Calf Woman then held the pipe before the chief, saying: "Behold this and always love it! It is very sacred and you must treat it as such. With this you will send your voices to Wakan Tanka, your father and grandfather."

The woman explained that the pipe represented the earth, and all plants and animals upon it. "When you pray with this pipe," she continued, "you pray for and with everything." White Buffalo Calf Woman gave the Sioux seven rites central to their religion, then showed them how to handle the pipe, pointing at the sky and the earth and toward the four winds. Then she wrapped the object in her bundle and gave it to the elderly chief. As she departed across the prairie, she turned into a white buffalo calf and disappeared over the horizon.

The pipe today is called Buffalo Calf Bone Pipe and—unlike most such relics, which have been destroyed or collected for display in museums—it is kept by the Sioux. Its stem is the lower leg of a buffalo calf, embellished with red eagle feathers, bird skins, and four small scalps. Brittle with age, the pipe is put away for safekeeping. Some Sioux say that the bundle will be opened only when the time is ripe for change, when an atmosphere of brotherhood and peace returns to the world.

Wherever a tribe's original pipe came from, it served as a model for replicas. They were often works of art, painstakingly crafted and elegantly decorated. The stem, of reed or wood, might be adorned with feathers, beads, and other symbolic ornament appropriate to a particular pipe's purpose. Among the Pawnee, the stem of a pipe used in war ceremonies was painted red and covered with the feathers of a male eagle; a peace pipe was painted blue and decorated with the feathers of a female eagle. Like many Indian peoples, the Pawnee carried their peace pipe with them on missions of conciliation to neighboring tribes. Two priests, charged with carrying the sacred wooden stem and stone bowl, traveled at the head of the procession wearing eagle feathers that symbolized their role as protectors of the tribe. When the Indians arrived at their destination, they took as one of their own a member of their hosts' village. This solemn act secured the peace.

Pipe bowls were usually made from soapstone, a mineral that is waterlogged underground and is easily worked after mining. Then it dries hard. The Sioux preferred a variety of soapstone called catlinite, red in

John Young Bear, a celebrated 20th-century Mesquakie artist, was known as a master carver of traditional wooden bowls, as well as an innovative designer of a number of other objects such as pipestems.

The typically sinuous shape of this Mesquakie bowl derives from the natural contours of the burl from which it was carved.

In the skilled hands of a Mesquakie carver, the curved blade, or "crooked knife," could be used to shape wooden bowls of delicate thinness.

THE HOLY GROVES

The Mesquakie believed the spirits of their ancestors dwelled within the trees of their Iowa homeland. "The murmur of the trees when the wind passes through is but the voices of our grandparents," explained one Mesquakie. The tribe, also known as the Fox Indians, thus considered wood and all objects made from wood to be sacred.

The wooden feast bowls used as ritual vessels during religious ceremonies were thought to contain the very essence of a tree's spiritual substance. The bowls ranged in size from a few inches to nearly two feet in diameter. The smallest were used for making medicine, the largest as serving vessels in the ceremonial lodge. They were carved from burls, the dense knotty outgrowths on tree trunks, that had been carefully hollowed out through a long process of burning and scraping.

Because their naturally rounded shape suggested the swelling of pregnancy, burls were looked upon as symbols of fertility. The bowls, which were endowed with the same associations, represented birth and were revered as symbols of hope for the continuity of the tribe.

color and quarried from a shallow vein in southwestern Minnesota. (The stone can also be found in Wisconsin and the Ohio River valley.) Legend explains that a huge flood once deluged ancient people living on the prairie, crushing them into the earth. Their flesh and bones turned into a pool of blood that, after a time, hardened into the sacred, crimson stone from which Indians carved their pipe bowls.

Although bowl shape and stem decoration vary widely between tribes, there is one feature of the sacred pipe that remains constant: Bowl and stem are always separate, just like the pipe brought to the Sioux by White Buffalo Calf Woman. A sacred pipe does not acquire religious power until the pieces are ceremonially joined together, and no one-piece pipe can be used to commune with the spirits. Native American craftsmen who make pipes for sale attach the bowl permanently to the stem. "In this way," explained two such artisans, "we make a personal statement to our people and to the public that our sacred objects are not for sale. To us, a pipe whose stem is detachable from the bowl is a spiritual tool, beyond being an art object."

Tobacco held special significance for the Crow Indians of Montana. The sacred leaf was so important to these buffalo-hunting nomads that tobacco societies sprang up within the tribe. Divided into chapters, these organizations devoted themselves to cultivating a special species of the plant for exclusive use in their own rituals. The Crows believed that simply growing this plant would bring good fortune, not only to society members but to the rest of the tribe as well.

Crow tobacco societies engaged in a complex cycle of planting, initiating new members, and harvesting the crop. During the winter months, those who were to join a chapter learned special songs and dances. As the soil warmed and the days grew longer, society elders met to discuss their dreams of the preceding winter, in which were revealed the best places for planting. After choosing auspicious plots, they prepared the tobacco seeds for sowing by mixing them with water—to soften them—and with roots and droppings of game animals. One day later, the entire tribe gathered at a central lodge for the planting ceremony.

Crow women played a major role in the tobacco-planting ritual, serving as bearers of the bags containing the venerable seed of the society's various chapters. After songs had been sung in honor of the plant, a woman carrying sacred medicine, such as an otter skin or pipe, would circle the lodge and lead the entire gathering outside. Then the group marched, single file, toward the designated planting spot. About 100

A Crow named Plain Owl holds a bird-headed staff used in his tribe's sacred Tobacco Ceremony. The tobacco cultivated in this ritual is not smoked but replanted yearly from its own seeds to reaffirm spiritual bonds. The Crows traditionally obtain smoking tobacco through trade.

yards short of their destination, everyone halted; the women handed their seed bags to the swiftest runners of each chapter, who raced with them to the garden plot. The winner could count on a healthy crop as well as good luck that year.

Officials of the tobacco society divided the planting ground among the chapters, then sent a young warrior, chosen earlier for his prowess in battle, to run across the plot and back again. This brief excursion symbolized participation in a war party. Afterward, the brave told how he had fought the enemy and that upon returning he found the tobacco flourishing. After proclaiming this encouraging report to the assembled tribe, an official wielding a stick feigned making a hole in the ground for the tobacco seeds. Three times he did this; then on the fourth, he stabbed a hole in the earth. Now the planting could begin.

Between planting and harvest, new members of the society were initiated. This ceremony, too, had a distinctive agenda of song, dance, and other ritual. The entire society—as well as those who were about to join—painted their faces with patterns revealed to them in personal visions. If a new member happened to have a vision of a design that already belonged to another society member, the initiate had to pay to use it. One youth is said to have paid his mother with a horse, money, quilts, and an ermine-skin shirt for the use of her design.

After tending the sacred plant through the spring and into the summer months, the societies harvested the tobacco when the wild cherries ripened. After gathering in the crop, they returned with it to the ceremonial lodge and danced with their bounty. Later, they ceremoniously shredded the leaves and twigs and threw them as an offering into the Missouri River, which the Crows believe to be one of the twins that created the universe and everything in it.

The use of tobacco to propitiate the spirits is a recurring theme in Native American tradition. Among the Ojibwa, the story is told of a young man who lived in a village at the foot of a peak, always obscured by clouds, that was said to be home to the thunderbirds, mythical creatures that made thunder and lightning. Hoping to see, or perhaps even capture

Members of the Crow tobacco society display their ceremonial robes trimmed with elk's teeth. Unlike most Indian sacred practices, the peaceful tobacco ritual was never formally banned by federal authorities. It continues to be performed, with the society still adopting new members, men and women, and holding annual ceremonies.

Holding evergreen boughs representing eternal life, the Indians of New Mexico's Santa Clara Pueblo perform the Corn Dance, a ritual prayer for rain, rich harvests, and general well-being. Commonly held during the summer months, corn dances may be performed at other times of the year to celebrate significant political or religious events that are taking place in the Pueblo.

a thunderbird, the young man decided to scale the mountain. He asked a friend to join him. As lacking in foresight as they were brash, the two friends set off, flouting the traditional admonition that no human should enter the realm of the spirits.

Thunder rumbled loudly as the pair approached the hidden crest, but above the din, the young climbers heard a strange chant: "Who dares without tobacco? Who dares without offering?" sang an unseen chorus. The brazen young man in search of the thunderbirds ignored the warning. As he stepped ahead of his friend into the mist, he shouted: "I see them! I see them!" Then, there was an earsplitting crack and a flash of light. In the eerie stillness that followed, the mist cleared, and the youth was seen tumbling down the mountain face to his death. So offended were the thunderbirds by his desecration that they abandoned the misty peak and were never heard there again.

Later, the survivor of the expedition was paddling his canoe in a lake at the base of the mountain. As he drew close to a foggy promontory, furious winds arose that whipped the water into a fearsome chop. Once again, he heard mysterious chanting. "Oh for the taste of tobacco! Oh for the smell of tobacco! Tobacco cleanses my heart," intoned a small, sad voice. Peering through the fog, the young man saw a tiny canoe carrying several people no larger than flowers, each holding a pipe.

Struggling to stay afloat in the rough water, the young man remembered the fate of his lost companion. He put aside his paddle, gathered up what tobacco he had with him, and tossed it onto the whitecapped waves. "Tobacco is our friend. Tobacco makes us friends," he called to the little men. Startled, they took the fragrant leaves from the water and filled their pipes. The mist cleared and the water calmed. No one ever saw the little people again, but ever since that day, the Ojibwa remember to offer tobacco where the spirits are thought to dwell.

A plant that was found almost as universally as tobacco among Native Americans was corn. Also known as maize, this nourishing grain constituted the Indians' most important food crop. First cultivated in Mexico around 5000 BC, corn enabled Indians to establish the complex village life that developed across the North American continent starting about 1500 BC. From the parched valleys of the Southwest to the luxuriant woodlands of the East, corn was perhaps the most sacred of all foods, the focus of countless legends and rituals.

With few exceptions, Indian legends about the origin of corn associ-

ate it with the fertility of women through a corn maiden or mother, or even a corn grandmother. Eastern tribes assigned the many tasks of growing and harvesting the crop mainly to women, who in this role bore much responsibility. An ample harvest meant plenty for all during the long winter months, while a poor yield could bring starvation. Although practices varied widely among tribes, women alone were believed to have the special power required to grow corn. Only women planted the crop. After working the soil and carefully placing seeds in small hillocks, an Iroquois woman might circle the field at night, pulling her clothing over the earth. Through this ritual, the Iroquois believed, she shared her fertility with the seeds.

"The Three Sisters," a 1937 watercolor by the Seneca artist Ernest Smith, personifies the corn, bean, and squash crops that constitute the traditional Iroquois diet. A benevolent elf (lower left) is turning the squash toward the sun to hasten its ripening. According to Iroquois legend, the helpful elves are also responsible for protecting the harvest from mildew, insects, and other blights.

Thousands of miles from the Iroquois, in the rugged Pueblo country of the Southwest, men planted the corn. Here, in a near-desert climate, a scarcity of game and wild fruit made the cultivation of corn truly a matter of life and death. So essential was the grain to southwestern tribes that the plant often influenced the structure of their society. The Tewa people divide themselves into winter people and summer people, each group presided over by a female corn spirit named for one of the colors that ears of corn take on as they ripen. Traditionally, Blue Corn Woman Near to Summer was responsible for summer people, who planted; White Corn Maiden Near to Ice took charge of winter people, who hunted.

Among the peoples of southwestern communities, the associations between corn and the supernatural permeated everyday life. Each extended family kept an ornately decorated ear of maize, which symbolized the well-being of the family. A corn plant was also placed on the cradleboard of a newborn infant to protect the child against threats ranging from snakes to witches. In a home where someone had died, an ear of maize held the ghosts of the departed during the traditional mourning period that lasted four days, then it was broken up and scattered on the grave. Ground into meal, maize became part of a daily sacrament; women sprinkled the fine powder over holy family possessions, such as animal fetishes, to nourish their spirits.

An annual cycle of ceremony frequently evolved to cajole and placate the spirits so that maize, beans, and other crops would grow. Not only in the Southwest but elsewhere, Indian peoples spoke to the spirits through song and dance, prayer and other ritual, in order to secure favorable planting and growing weather.

For many tribes, winter was a spiritual time. During these dark and quiet months, with grain stores low and game scarce, Native Americans reassured themselves through communication with the spirit world. Noting that the sun crosses the sky nearer the southern horizon as winter approaches, many Indian tribes exhorted the sun to return northward and warm the earth for corn to grow. Of all such ceremonies, the one evolved by the Hopi was perhaps the most elaborate. Called the Soyal, it was held at the winter solstice—the shortest day of the year, and the one on which the sun reverses its southward retreat. The purpose was nothing less than to change the course of the sun.

Many days in advance, Hopi priests prayed and readied the kiva. Built below ground level, this circular temple, where the ritual would be enacted, was close to the subterranean domain of the spirits, from which the people had risen in mythological times. During this period of preparation, the priests avoided all meat, as well as grease and salt. Such abstinence, it was believed, would keep their thoughts pure. On the kiva floor, the priests sprinkled cornmeal, sand, and colored powders made from bark as well as flowers arranged in patterns that symbolized the universe. Surrounded by corn ears and other holy objects, the floor design would be used as an altar. The holy men also

This headband made from a duck skin with the bill attached was worn by a woman of the Hidatsa Goose Society, whose members had the power to make gardens flourish and ensure successful harvests. Their crops were treated as tenderly as human offspring. As one Hidatsa woman explained in 1921: "We thought that the corn plants had souls, as children had souls."

crafted feathered rods that served as prayer sticks for sending messages to the spirits. Like the tobacco smoke through which they were passed, feathers were thought to assist spiritual communication.

As the day of the ceremony approached, messengers visited every Hopi home carrying cornhusk "boats" filled with cornmeal that had prayer feathers inserted around the perimeter. Corn pollen was sprinkled in the center, also to carry prayers. Collected the preceding year, the pollen symbolized fertility. Each man, woman, and child breathed upon these husks and prayed over them. After the husks were returned to the kiva, messengers again passed through the village, this time collecting precious kernels of seed corn drawn from the central repository by the women of the tribe, who were charged with preserving the seeds for planting. They were placed on an altar in the kiva and sprinkled with earth. Thus sanctified, they were returned to the storehouse. The blessing conferred upon the seed at the altar would spread to the other kernels, helping to ensure an ample crop.

Hopi men dressed as rain-giving kachina spirits gather for the February ceremony called the Powamu. Also known as the Bean Dance, the Powamu is a 16-day-long collection of rites meant to spiritually prepare the Hopi's arid land for the planting season. Beans are sprouted in boxes of moist sand. Their growth in the hothouselike warmth of a kiva, a semisubterranean ceremonial house, portends the future harvest.

At the solstice, the entire village entered the kiva for the final Soyal rites that would alter the sun's path and renew the cycle of seasons. This feat was to be accomplished by a kachina—a man who, upon donning a mask, became one of the myriad spirits that animated the Hopi world. The Soyal kachina wore symbols of the heavens, his face dotted with white paint and his head crowned by a cornhusk star. In one hand he carried a shield, edged with feathers, to represent the sun. As he whirled about the kiva waving his shield, the kachina sought to impart the energy the sun would need to make its arduous journey toward summer.

With warming weather, the Hopi enacted other ceremonies intended to secure favorable planting conditions. When it was time to sow, another round of ritual ensured that the seeds would sprout and thrive. This final sequence centered on Masau, the god of life and death and the most powerful spirit on earth. Masau smeared his face with rabbit blood and streaked it with black paint. Over his head and face, he wore the skin of a freshly killed rabbit, fur-side in. The spirit's body, also painted with blood, was attired in both a man's loincloth and a woman's dress to symbolize his power over everything. A belt of corn ears ringed his waist. For four nights before planting, Masau ran around the village to consecrate the space. Each night he ran in a smaller circle in order to bring the rain clouds nearer. On planting day, Masau performed antics to encourage the kernels as they lay in the soil. First he would hide in the furrowed earth and spring out suddenly, chasing the planters gathered in the field. Then he would dash about, striking people with a small sack of cotton. The blows reminded the people that life was hard. The cotton symbolized the clouds floating through the sky bringing rain.

Just as complex as the Hopi ceremony was the rainmaking ritual of the Papago of Arizona, whose short growing season required a timely infusion of water. The Papago could not plant crops until midsummer, when the vast blue sky filled with clouds and rain slaked the parched earth. Except during this brief season of planting and harvest, the Papago lived by hunting game and foraging.

Papago rainmaking depended on the towering saguaro cactus. From the crimson fruit of the saguaro, the Papago brewed a liquor, which they drank in a ritual celebration. Imbibing this alcoholic syrup, the Papago believed, would encourage the rains to saturate the earth.

Each family owned a cactus grove. When the fruit was ripe, the women covered the ground beneath the cactus plants with canvas and knocked the spiny, plumlike fruit to the ground with a hook that was mounted on the end of a pole made of saguaro ribs. After collecting the fruit, they boiled it in clay jars and took the brew to a council house. There, a priest and the elders of the tribe watched over the fermenting juice, which was believed to have the power to draw good wind and clouds. For up to four days and nights, the men waited for bubbles of carbon dioxide to form in the holy liquid, creating a froth that symbolized clouds and rain. Outside, the village took turns singing and dancing solemnly around a fire to aid the process.

Toward dawn between the third and fifth day, the village priests announced that the beverage was ready, whereupon the ceremonial drinking of the liquor commenced. Four holy men sat in a circle marking the directions of the four winds. The rest of the village men sat around them in an enormous circle. Prayers or chants followed, inviting everyone to take the liquid as they prayed that rain would soak the earth. Next, eight young men carried the liquor from the council house to the villagers outside. The holy men drank first. As the pulpy red beverage passed around

Three women from southern Arizona's Maricopa tribe stand beside a cluster of giant saguaro cactus holding the bowls they use to gather the fruit that sprouts on the plant's spiny limbs in early summer. The plum-sized fruit, brewed into a ritual liquor by the neighboring Papago for their annual rainmaking ceremonies, heralds the southwestern desert's brief growing season.

As part of a four-day-long puberty rite, a young Apache girl is showered with yellow pollen from the tule, a southwestern cattail rush. Tule pollen was the Apache's most powerful medicine, administered to heal the sick and wounded, sprinkled on crops to ensure their growth, and painted on moccasins to help travelers find their way.

the circle, the men prayed that it would bring wind and clouds. When the skies opened—as they do every afternoon during the rainy season, no matter how briefly—the Papago knew that their magic had once again succeeded.

Although southwestern tribes placed greater emphasis than others on bringing rain—even the taking of scalps figured in the process—most communities across North America practiced similar rites, just as they all celebrated the reappearance of nature's bounty every summer. Prominent among these so-called first fruits rites was the Green Corn Ceremony, which was performed at the time when kernels formed behind tender husks.

In this ritual as in other first fruits ceremonies, the people acknowledged the spiritual source of the game, fruit, and vegetables they ate and gave thanks for their return. Such practices originated with the Indians' hunter-gatherer forebears, who exalted the season's edibles before partaking of them.

Sacraments that were customarily associated with the green corn rite included stern dietary restrictions. In addition to observing a ban on eating any of the crop until appropriate rituals had been performed, planting tribes also usually did penance by refraining from eating salt in the days leading up to a green corn ceremony. To take salt, to violate any other taboo, or to ignore the prescribed ritual preparations for eating the new corn could endanger the harvest. Disease and ill fortune would surely follow.

Among the Creek Indians, who lived originally in present-day Georgia and Alabama before being displaced to Oklahoma, the Green Corn Ceremony reaches a peak in the so-called Busk, a ritual that is performed to this day. Traditionally, in preparation for the ceremony, women and children scoured the dwellings and even extinguished the household fires that had been kept burning continuously since the preceding year's Busk. In the meantime, the men prepared the square where the Busk would be held, scraping away a layer of earth and sprinkling fresh soil, or sometimes white sand, over the area. Four logs specially chosen for a ceremonial fire were laid in the center, with a timber pointing in each of the cardinal directions. (From this blaze, the women would later take coals to rekindle hearth fires.) After the consecration of the square, no one could enter who had not fasted.

The first day of a Busk, which usually lasted four days, was one of purification. Gathering in the square, the men settled or forgave all debts and quarrels of the preceding year; no substantial harvest could be expected in the absence of harmony among tribe members. Shirkers and tribe members guilty of other antisocial behavior atoned for their acts by confessing and asking forgiveness. Even a murderer who had escaped execution by fleeing into the forest would be absolved if he could reach the square unharmed during a Busk.

Next came the ritual designed to bring about bodily purification. A medicine man prepared the ceremonial black drink, an oily tea brewed mainly from the leaves and twigs of holly bushes. As each man prepared to take a swallow, a priest gave a sharp high-pitched bark. Several times throughout the day, the rite was repeated; some participants made themselves vomit to eject any evil within them.

During the next three days, men and women performed a variety of dances, sometimes separately, sometimes together. During a dance extolling womanhood, for example, women performed alone, dressed in their best clothing and wearing turtle-shell rattles at the ankle. In Creek legend, turtles hold up the world, and the turtle shells proclaim women the foundation of society. The dancers also carried knives to indicate their willingness to prepare food for their men. Accompanied by a singer, the women walked four times around the square. The men performed the Buffalo Dance, carrying sticks in both hands to make themselves four-legged like the animals they revered. After the dancing, the participants gathered for a purifying bath in a nearby stream.

The ban on eating new corn was now over. A few young ears were offered to the ceremonial fire in the village square. Then, the milky kernels were set before a priest, who prayed for a plentiful yield, and a great feast of corn and fresh game ensued.

By means of rites such as the Busk, Indians renewed the partnership that had long existed between humans and supernatural beings. The spirits, the Indians believed, had done their share by providing corn. Now it was time for humankind to balance the equation through ritual. In addition, it was thought that the forces of nature tended to decline through inactivity, like a battery running down. Unless something was done to recharge these powers, the animals would vanish, the plants would fade, and the people would starve.

Striving to harmonize their lives with the natural world, Native Americans turned to the earth's green carpet for help in healing. Indians used a huge array of botanicals as cures. One survey of herbal medicines listed 68 laxatives, 88 cold remedies, and 113 plants for reducing fever. Beyond that, 41 plants were recommended for nervous ailments, and more than 100 relieved an upset stomach. Crushed leaves of the tulip tree might be applied to a patient's face, for example, to soothe a headache. Pine bark was boiled and then applied as a salve to burns; catnip tea was given to infants to alleviate colic and gas pains. And sassafras was a panacea, used for everything from scurvy to spring fever.

Like tobacco and food crops, medicinal plants were considered gifts from the spirit world. Cherokee legend gives an explanation for the power of plants to cure disease. According to the story, humans and animals lived together in peace and even spoke to one another. But humans began to multiply rapidly. Facing starvation, the people not only crowded their four-footed friends into forests, but began slaughtering their former allies for hides and furs as well as food, greatly reducing their numbers. For this abuse, the animals

Medicinal plants and roots once owned by a Sioux woman are kept wrapped in paper and muslin and stored in a painted rawhide case. The plants were ground into powders and then steeped in water to produce curative teas.

took revenge. At the suggestion of the deer tribe, they resolved that a human must offer a prayer each time he took the life of an animal. Failure to do so would bring disease. Upon learning this, the plant kingdom took pity on the humans. Trees, grasses, shrubs, and herbs decided to offer themselves as cures for ailments created by the animals. Forever afterward, it was believed, the spirits of plants would provide proper remedies for various diseases.

These remedies were often closely guarded secrets, passed from one family or healer to another with great reverence. Cures were thought to work largely through the cooperation of the spirit world, and herbal healers went to great lengths to fortify their medicines through religious rites. Complex organizations, such as the Midewiwin, or Grand Medicine Society, of the Ojibwa and other Great Lakes tribes evolved to perform, among other responsibilities, the important tasks of selecting and applying herbal cures. These healers—who might be men or women—had special abilities to communicate with plant spirits.

Like many other Native American tribes, the Delaware, or Lenape, Indians chose herbalists from among those members with a special affinity for the plant kingdom, as revealed in a vision. One Lenape healer, whose powers earned her the name Touching Leaves Woman, had such an experience when she was a small child. She was riding a horse with her aunt through deep woods, when the older woman fell unconscious on the ground. It was evening, and the little girl was terrified by the deepening forest shadows. Suddenly, she saw the trees become almost human. As a breeze gently stirred their leaves, they smiled and spoke kindly to her, promising that no harm would befall her.

They kept their pledge. The girl and her aunt were soon found, and the older woman recovered completely. To Touching Leaves Woman's people, the young girl's connection with plant spirits was clear, and the tribe had no doubt that she would learn the secrets of their roots, leaves, and stems to heal her people.

Lenape herbalists, men and women, followed rigorous procedures when collecting ingredients and compounding their remedies. Before even searching for a botanical remedy, the herbalists would pray to the supreme power for assistance in healing the stricken person. Next, tobacco would be offered, a pinch tossed over the shoulder in the direction of each of the four winds. The healers needed the force of the wind spirits to add power to their nostrums. When the herbalists located the curative species, they offered tobacco once more, this time by placing a handful in a small hole that had been scooped out on the east side of the stalk. The gift enlisted the support of the herb's spirit, which was essential to its effectiveness. Finally, the healers offered a prayer to the plant.

In collecting their vegetal remedies, Lenape herbalists adhered to strict taboos. A menstruating woman, for example, would never gather herbs; she was believed to have natural powers in her own right that would interfere with the power of the plant. If herbalists encountered a sign of bad luck while gathering plants—a poisonous snake crossing the path, for example—they would imme-

HYDRANGEA ARBORESCENS (WILD HYDRANGEA)

According to Cherokee belief, all the plants of the earth, from the trees and shrubs to the humblest mosses, were responsible for curing specific human ills, making the entire plant kingdom a vast natural pharmacopoeia. Tribal medicine men typically were familiar with the curative powers of some 400 plant species, recognizing, for example, that the bark of the wild hydrangea (left) could be chewed to quiet a troubled stomach, mashed into a poultice for sore muscles, or brewed into a tea to stop a child's vomiting. The root of the dwarf iris (below), when pulverized and mixed with hog's lard, beef suet, and beeswax, made a salve for sores. Liquid taken from the root of the black-eyed Susan (right, top) relieved earaches, while a tea brewed from its root made a healing lotion for sores and snakebites or a drink that could remedy dropsy. Potions made from the root of the versatile lady's-slipper (right, bottom) relieved muscle spasm, fits, hysteria, and pain, as well as the symptoms of flu and the common cold.

diately return home and avoid working with medicines for the rest of the day. Picking the first plant discovered in the search was also proscribed; the Lenape and other tribes believed that this find must remain untouched to convey the herbalist's prayer to others of the species. Only in this way would the plants know what was asked of them.

Preparing the remedy required equally close attention to detail. Roots and leaves were placed in the sun to dry, since solar rays were thought to fortify a plant's medicinal qualities. If water was required to brew a medicine, the herbalist would draw it from a stream; flowing-water spirits were thought to be stronger than those of a pond or lake. In mixing a solution, a Lenape herb doctor was careful to stir in a clockwise direction, imitating the sun's path across the sky to enlist the sun spirit's aid. Blowing on a hot liquid to lower the temperature was forbidden; doing so was thought to offend the spirit of the plant, which did not like the suggestion that the mixture was cooling too slowly at its own pace.

The Lenape and other tribes sometimes used herbs to work bad medicine or evil as well as to heal. In these cases, a powerful sorcerer worked the magic. He would collect the plant in much the same manner as the herbalist, careful to speak to its spirit as ritual demanded and not to take

IRIS CRISTATA (DWARF IRIS)

**RUDBECKIA FULGIDA
(BLACK-EYED SUSAN)**

the first sample he happened across. Speaking grimly to the plant spirit, he repeated the name of his victim several times as he vigorously dug up the herb, scattering as much dirt as possible. By these actions, the shaman indicated that he wanted his victim shown no mercy. Immersing the plant among the powerful spirits in a stream, he roughly pulled off the roots while again intoning the name of his prey.

This act was thought to magically transform the roots into the victim. At this point, the sorcerer might utter a curse of poverty or some other affliction as he flung the roots into the stream. Or with the intent of turning the hapless individual into an alcoholic, he might immerse them in a small bottle of whiskey. In a variation, the sorcerer could secrete an evil charm where the victim might pass, perhaps to frighten his horse in the hope of causing him injury. Bad medicine such as this could only be overcome by a powerful herb doctor with secret potions at his disposal.

Other Indian peoples have used plants in similar ways to exert influence. Herbs were employed to attract fish and game, or to ensure safety and success. A traveler might carry a root that had been given special power to keep him from danger; dried flowers might be placed on coals to make fumes that could ward off an evil curse.

One of the notable practitioners of such spiritual endeavors with plants was Mourning Dove, a woman belonging to the Okanagon tribe in northwestern Washington State whose life of some 60 years bridged the turn of the 20th century. A spokeswoman for her people among whites, she also recorded details of her life and the ways of her tribe. One of her clearest memories was of the love charm described by her grandmother.

Perhaps recognizing that the teenager possessed special abilities, Mourning Dove's grandmother sought to impart to her the secrets of herbal spells at the time that she was 14 years old. Taking her granddaughter far into the mountains, the old woman showed Mourning Dove a small pool edged with dainty yellow flowers,

**CYPRIPEDIUM ACAULE
(LADY'S-SLIPPER)**

which, she told her, could be used to secure the affection of a husband.

Following the death of her grandmother, Mourning Dove went in search of another herbalist who would teach her about love charms; she found such a woman among a branch of the tribe living in British Columbia. In time, the two traveled together on horseback into the mountains, and after conducting rituals of purification, they happened upon a tiny spring fringed by yellow and white flowers. The older woman prayed, talking to the plants: "You are great—the spirit of the earth. I pray for your help. The sun shines upon you, and the brook sings your song with me this day. I beg that my work be a success." She showed Mourning Dove how to join lovers by tying a female plant to a male plant and putting the bound pair back in the earth. (To separate lovers, she explained, tear apart the roots of intertwined plants.) Then she tucked into a buckskin bag a bit of root that she sliced from a similar plant nearby.

After they had returned home, the woman fashioned a love charm for Mourning Dove's use. In addition to the root, it included bits of bear tongue, beaver, doves, hummingbirds, robins, and crickets. Each ingredient served a specific purpose—the beaver, for example, lent wisdom to the charm, while the crickets, because of the chirping sound they made when alive, made it alluring to its intended victims. These ingredients were crushed into a fine powder and placed in the buckskin bag.

Mourning Dove tested the effectiveness of the love charm on men she found proud and disdainful, and claimed some success. Then one day when a funeral procession passed near where Mourning Dove had hidden the charm, it lost its efficacy and she had to put it aside. Over the years, however, she became increasingly convinced of the charm's ancient power. "The spiritual herbs are blessings that God bestowed upon our ancestors," she wrote in her autobiography. "I am now more sure than ever that our ancient Indian wisdom and knowledge are the surest source of safety, salvation, and success in life."

Exotic macaw feathers are combined with the plumage of domestic birds in a peyote fan. A tiny cross hanging from the fringe reflects Christian influences on the peyote ritual.

At sunset, the worshipers gather in the tipi to honor the Great Spirit and all the lesser spirits, through the medium of Grandfather Peyote. Around the perimeter of the tipi they sit, backs erect, facing an earthen altar where a sacramental peyote button rests in a slender furrow. So holy is this particular plant that it is never eaten and is passed from generation to generation. Each man consumes his share of peyote, the young men choosing the rubbery, dusky green buttons while the elders swallow a powder of crushed peyote. The hours pass. By midnight it is time to sip water, to moisten parched tongues.

With the arrival of that hour, the still air over the tipi is pierced by four sharp blasts from an eagle-bone whistle, and a young woman enters the tipi carrying a bucket of water. She pauses respectfully and waits until the ceremonial leader has given her a blessing before she brings the water forward. After each of the worshipers has taken four swallows, the woman departs, and the sounds of the ceremony resume: the steady pulse of a drum, the gentle shake of rattles, the murmur of song rising and falling in the language of prayer.

Delaware Indians in Oklahoma conduct peyote rites around the crescent-shaped sand altar inside a tipi. Peyote fans and gourd rattles are shaken to accompany the singing of vision songs, contributing color, movement, and a soft percussive sound.

Throughout the night and onward until dawn, a ceremonial official tends the glowing embers at the tipi's center, where four logs have been placed, pointing in the directions of the four winds. Another official burns cedar incense, symbol of the earth's greenery. The worshipers smoke tobacco, hand-rolled into cornhusk wrappers. For many hours, the men sit still, alert and peaceful, welcoming the visions that arise from the fire's smoke and creep in through the tipi flap. At dawn the ceremony ends; the men feast on sweetened meat, dried corn, and fruit. They leave the tipi and rest in a shady spot, content in the knowledge that they have renewed their partnership with the spirits.

Peyote, a small, spineless cactus that is native to Mexico, was first employed by the Indians living in northern Mexico as a mild hallucinogen during rituals, and it is an ancient Aztec legend that relates how the cactus first came to the Indians. A young woman heavy with child was foraging for roots with her people when her labor began. Falling behind, she gave birth alone in the desert. Exhausted and frightened, she lay near a low bush with her child.

Unable to care for herself or her infant, the woman was awaiting death when she heard the voice of a spirit that said, "Eat the plant that is growing beside you. That is life and blessing for you and all your people." Next to her she found a small cactus. The young woman pulled it up by the roots and ate the small, round head. She revived immediately, her breasts filling with milk. After having nursed her newborn, she set out to try to find her people, taking with her as much of the cactus as she was able to carry. By that evening, she and her child had rejoined the tribe. The woman showed the strange new plants to her uncle, a wise man who was able to understand their power. "This is truly a blessing," he announced. "We must give it to all the people." Thereafter, a body of ritual grew up around peyote, and long before it came to the United States in the mid-1800s, the cactus had become the principal sacrament of a well-established religion south of the border.

Although the first appearance of peyote ritualism in America is undocumented, the early spread of the religion has two origins. One was Moon Head, a Caddo Indian from Oklahoma who was better known as John Wilson. Later and independently, a Comanche named Quanah Parker, son of a Comanche chief and a white woman captured as a little girl and raised as an Indian, learned of the religion from a Mexican herbal healer after he fell ill on a visit to his long-lost white grandparents in Texas. Wilson and Parker shared their versions of the new religion, which

Photographed in the 1920s, Eaves Tall Chief, an Osage Indian, sits stiffly in front of a painted studio backdrop holding a peyote fan and rattle. Introduced to the southern Plains in the 1840s, rituals that were based upon peyote eventually spread north into southern Canada and as far east as the Great Lakes region.

differed largely in the length of the ceremony, first with close friends and then with other Indian leaders, who blended in their own rituals.

For Native Americans living in the late 1800s, the peyote ritual also turned out to be a blessing. During two short centuries of contact with Europeans, the Indian way of life had been ravaged. Nowhere was this felt more deeply than on the Great Plains, where once-mighty buffalo herds had been wiped out taking much of the Indian culture with them. On the Plains and across the continent, Indian spiritual life was under attack. "White people say that our dances and our songs are not good," said a Pima Indian of that era.

In 1890, following a violent attack by the U.S. Army on unarmed Sioux at Wounded Knee, many Indians turned to the new peyote faith. Before the tragedy the ritual had enjoyed only modest success in attracting followers. Afterward, it seemed to offer spiritual solace that all could appreciate. Not only did the cactus rituals embody the spiritual link to nature that Indians valued, but the spirit of peyote also demanded abstinence from liquor and a kind and generous attitude toward others. Furthermore, the hallucinogenic properties of the cactus made eating it a substitute for the traditional vision quest, which provoked visions through a combination of strongly held belief, physical deprivation, psychological isolation, and sometimes self-torture. This kind of search for a spiritual identity had been discouraged by the officials of the government.

Beginning around 1900 and for many years thereafter, federal alcohol laws against selling liquor to Indians were applied indiscriminately to peyote, even though the applicable statutes made no mention of the cactus. At length, peyote priests found an answer to their dilemma. They would legitimize their faith by chartering it in each state. Oklahoma granted the first such charter to the new religion, called The Native American Church, in 1918. Since then, the church has been recognized in many states, from California to New York.

The use of peyote, however, remains illegal in many jurisdictions, and church members who partake of it risk prosecution. In spite of that possibility, the peyote rite continues to win converts among Native Americans who yearn for a connection to their ancient spiritual past. For many of them, the humble cactus is emblematic of the longstanding spiritual connection that has always existed between the Indians and the plants of their world—including the knowledge that corn came at great sacrifice from the gods, and the certainty that a spiral of tobacco smoke carries the hopes of the people directly to the spirits. ❖

HEALING WAYS OF THE NAVAJO

The essence of Navajo culture is the maintenance of *hózhǫ́,* a term that corresponds roughly to the English word *harmony.* Wrong behavior of any kind can upset the delicate balance between the good and evil powers in the Navajo universe and bring sickness and misfortune to the transgressor. To restore the disrupted order and treat the diseases, the Navajo possess myriad ancient healing ceremonies, called Chant Ways. Each Way is so complex that a practitioner, or singer, rarely masters more than two of them in a lifetime. A single Way can last up to nine days or longer and involve many prayers, medicines, and offerings, as well as hundreds of songs that recount Navajo history. The ceremony may also involve the creation of several dry, or sand, paintings, selected from the dozens used in the Chant Ways.

These paintings are made primarily of colored sandstone ground into a fine powder. The singer and his assistants trickle the pigment onto a bed of fresh sand on the floor of the patient's hogan. The patient, bearing a gift of cornmeal, sits on the painting, facing east, the direction from which all Navajo blessings come. Attracted by the ceremony, the relevant supernatural powers enter the painting and make it their home. If the powers are pleased, the patient is cured. Afterward, the singer's assistants ceremonially dispose of the sand, which has absorbed the evil that caused the disharmony. The examples on the following pages, each one shown with the direction east at the top, were made for documenting the ceremonial designs. Sand paintings actually used in the healing rituals are considered too sacred to be photographed.

This masked dancer, portraying a "yé'ii," one of the many deities in the Navajo pantheon, carries the sacred paraphernalia he will use in the Nightway ritual.

WATERWAY

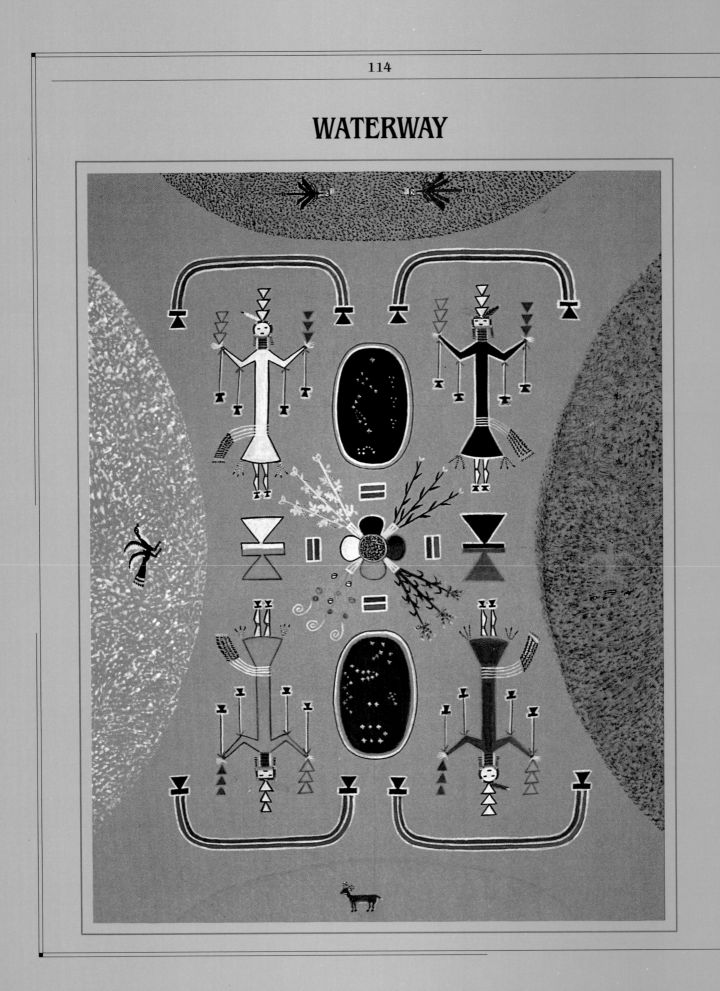

SHOOTINGWAY

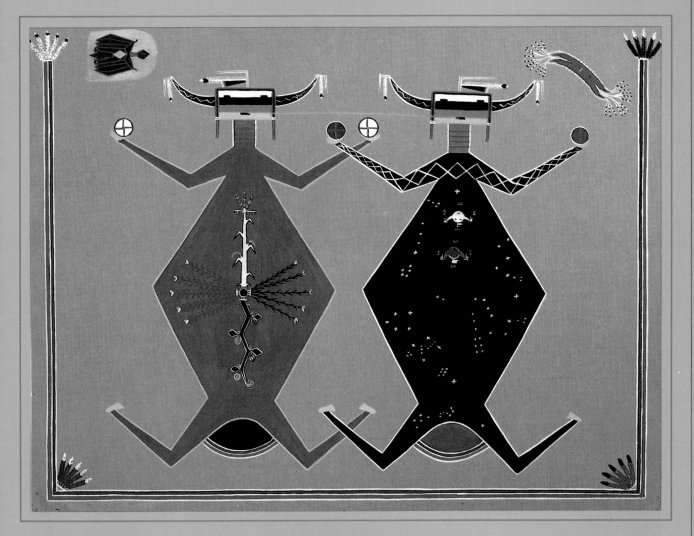

Emergence Lake, the route through which the Navajo ascended to this world, occupies the center of the sand painting shown at left. Stalks from the four sacred plants—corn, squash, beans, and tobacco—radiate from its sides. The elongated figures are Rain People, who are carrying clouds. They flank the east and west oceans (ovals at center), whose surfaces reflect the stars.

Mother Earth (above left) and Father Sky, two of the most powerful Navajo deities, dominate this sand painting, a design made on the fourth day of a healing ceremony called Shootingway that addresses respiratory and gastro-intestinal diseases. Mother Earth contains the sacred plants and a spring of water. Father Sky contains the sun, the moon, and several constellations, including the Milky Way. A thin yellow line of pollen, symbolizing positive energy, unites the rectangular heads of the two deities.

EARTHWAY

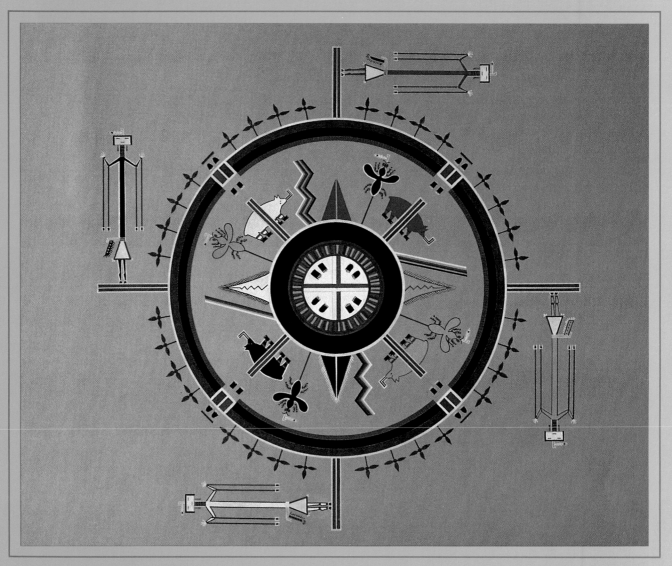

Bears, thought by the Navajo to possess healing powers, appear in each of the quadrants of this sand painting, a design created for an Earthway ritual intended to restore a woman to harmony with the world around her. The inner circles at the center of the painting are the home of the bears and also represent the dawn. The black and yellow Holy People are the male Gods Who Hold Up the Earth; the blue and white Holy People are the female Gods Who Hold Up the Sky. The patient is fed digested honey from the intestines of a bear, and sometimes her body is rubbed with sand from a bear's paw print to give her strength.

This sand painting from Blessingway, the most important Navajo ceremony, shows their homeland as a square flanked by ovals representing the four sacred mountains. Inside the square are Changing Woman (top), who represents nature and the mystery of reproduction, and her sister, White Shell Woman, who represents water. The central circle is the place of emergence. The line running from the yellow oval is the reed through which the First People arose from the underworld.

BLESSINGWAY

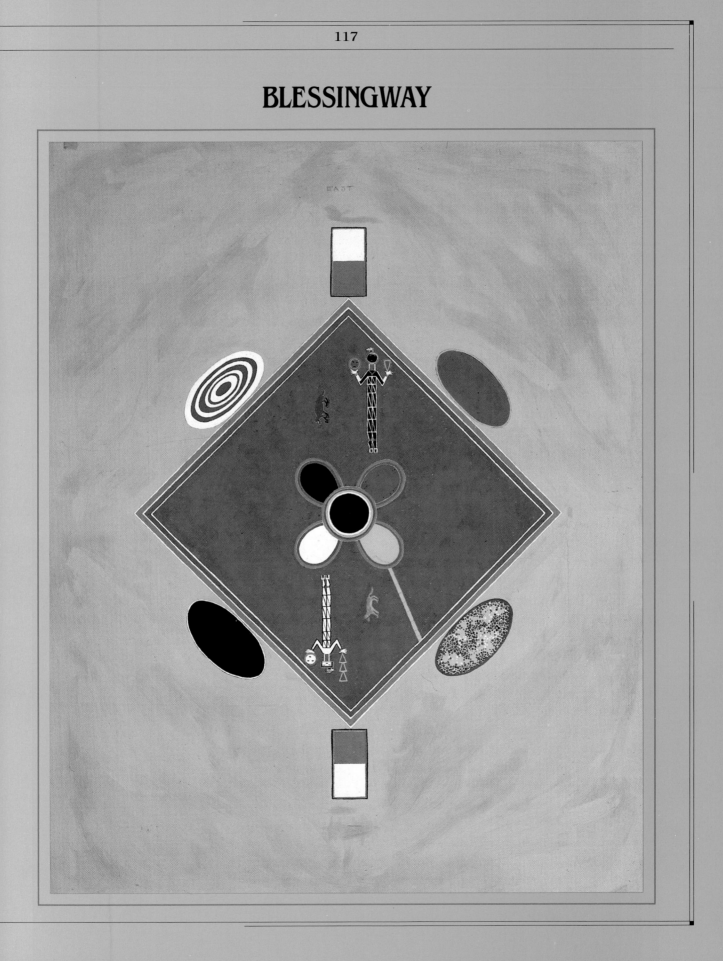

PAINTING WITH SAND

Navajo artist Joe Ben, Jr., takes traditional sand painting designs from the tribal healing rituals and reinterprets them as contemporary art. Although his paintings are permanent works created strictly for their beauty, Ben believes that they nevertheless contain beneficial power. "The energy is there," he says, "but the viewer must turn the key for it to be released."

Ben practices many of the age-old techniques used in the Navajo ceremonies, grinding up colored rocks for pigment and carefully trickling it onto the painting with his fingers. But instead of using a hogan floor, as is the custom during the Navajo healing rituals, he works at a table, employs many nontraditional materials, and fixes the granules in place by means of glue.

Ben breaks up brightly colored rocks found in the Southwest. His favorites, at the bottom of these pages, are white gypsum, red sandstone, and the turquoise stone chrysocolla. He also uses nontraditional minerals, such as copper ore, coal shale, and diamond and gold dust.

Ben pulverizes a chunk of red sandstone on a grinding stone. For harder minerals, he uses a hand-operated corn grinder. He makes granules of different sizes to create different textures.

Having applied a narrow strip of adhesive to make the pigment adhere, Ben drips granules of chrysocolla onto the headdress of a Navajo thunderbird.

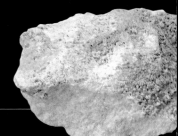

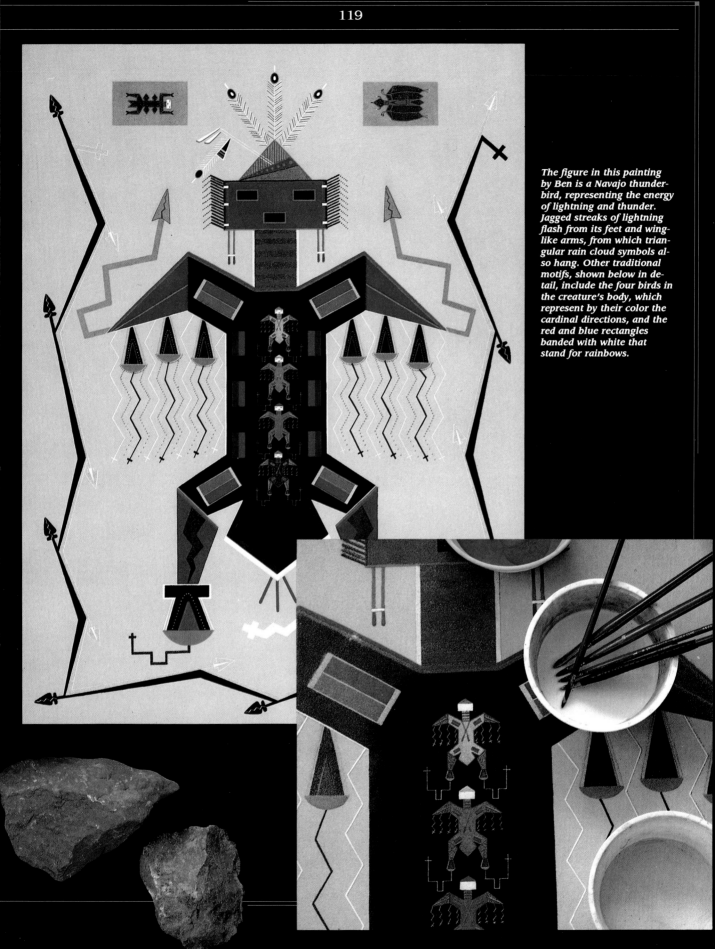

The figure in this painting by Ben is a Navajo thunderbird, representing the energy of lightning and thunder. Jagged streaks of lightning flash from its feet and wing-like arms, from which triangular rain cloud symbols also hang. Other traditional motifs, shown below in detail, include the four birds in the creature's body, which represent by their color the cardinal directions, and the red and blue rectangles banded with white that stand for rainbows.

4

CRYING FOR A VISION

On the vast plains of North Dakota, a Mandan shaman lifts a bleached buffalo skull skyward as part of a ritual to ensure a successful hunt. One of the traditional roles of the shaman has been to commune with wild animals and beseech them to act as friends to humankind.

One morning, an hour or so after dawn, a young Oglala Sioux climbed purposefully through the fir trees that carpet the Black Hills of South Dakota. A buffalo robe was draped over one arm, and he held a pipe in front of him. Its bowl was sealed with tallow so that it could not be smoked. The youth walked with the resolute step of one who knew exactly where he had to go and what he had to do. He had set off on the age-old quest known to his people as *hanbleceya,* or crying for a vision—an ordeal performed by most Sioux males as a means of establishing personal contact with Wakan Tanka, the Great Mystery.

Helpers had gone before him, and when the young Indian arrived at his hilltop destination, he found that they had prepared the site carefully. Five wooden poles had been planted in the ground. The outer shafts, aligned with the four cardinal points of the compass, stood about 10 paces from a center post that symbolized the upper and lower worlds of the Sioux universe. A bundle of sacred objects, wrapped in hide, adorned each pole, and a pinch of kinnikinnick, a powerful mixture of tobacco, various grasses, bearberries, and shavings from the inner bark of trees, had been placed beneath the center pole. The bed of sage that they had laid on the ground for him to rest on stretched eastward from the center pole so that when the youth awoke in the morning, he would be facing the rising sun. After completing their work, the assistants had ridden back to the village. The young man was alone with the woods and the sky.

In accordance with ancient ritual, the youth went directly to the center pole, then turned westward to look at the rolling hills. Holding the pipe in both hands, he cried out to Wakan Tanka to take pity on him that his people might live. Over the hours that followed, the vision seeker repeated the cry many times, both aloud and silently, as he walked in an exceedingly slow and respectful manner between the poles, delivering his prayer first to the west, then to the north, the east, and the south, returning each time to the center post. After completing a few rounds, he raised his pipe in supplication to the sky. Then, pointing the pipe to the ground, he begged assistance from the earth.

Throughout the day, the youth kept careful watch over every living

Imposing mountain peaks, rock formations, and a lake made this secluded corner of Bighorn Canyon in southern Montana a favorite site for the Crow Indians who were seeking to experience a vision. Despite the flooding of the canyon following the construction of a dam, Crow people continue to find inspiration in its majestic landscape.

thing that shared the solitude of his aerie. He knew that Wakan Tanka usually manifested itself in the form of animals or birds. A chance sighting of a squirrel, a hawk, or an eagle might provide a revelation. The seeker would know if he heard the creature speak. It might give him a message or, if he was truly fortunate, teach him the words of a song.

Well after the last light had drained away behind the hills, the young man continued to pace between the poles, repeating his plea to the starlit sky. Even when fatigue finally overcame him and he lay down to rest on his scented bed of sage, he did not give up the quest, for he knew that the most powerful visions often come in dreams. He arose from time to time during the night to resume his prayers, and before dawn broke he was up again, raising his pipe in silent offering to the morning star. The ordeal extended through another day and night. As the hours dragged past, fatigue and hunger heightened his perception. With neither food nor drink to sustain him, it was as though his body and brain were being emptied to receive the divine light.

At the end of the appointed time, the helpers returned with horses to carry the young man back to camp. By then he was lightheaded with hunger and lack of sleep, and at times, they had to steady him on his mount to save him from falling. Although the helpers burned with curiosity, tradition prescribed that they refrain from questioning him, and the young man kept his silence all the way back to the village where he was ushered into the presence of the holy man to whom he had made his vow.

"You have now sent a voice with your pipe to Wakan Tanka," the holy man said. "That pipe is now very sacred, for the whole universe has seen it. And since you are about to put this pipe to your mouth, you should tell us nothing but the truth. The pipe is Wakan and knows all things; you cannot fool it."

The holy man removed the tallow, filled the bowl with kinnikinnick, and lighted it with a coal from the fire. After the pipe had been offered to the powers of the six directions of the universe and passed around the circle of listeners four times, the quester began his report. Several eagles had flown near him, he said, but said nothing. A red-breasted woodpecker, however, had alighted on one of the offering poles, and he had heard the bird say faintly yet distinctly: "Be attentive and have no fear; but pay no attention to any bad thing that may come and talk to you." Later on, he saw the morning star change color, from red to blue to yellow to white. Then, just before the end of his vigil, the woodpecker returned and spoke clearly to him: "Friend, be attentive as you walk."

THE WONDERS IN A DREAM

While riding along the Little Bighorn River one day in 1873, a nine-year-old Oglala boy later named Black Elk collapsed from a mysterious illness that would leave him unconscious for 12 days. While he lay inert in a tipi, he had a vision: Two cloud-borne men came before him singing, "All over the sky a sacred voice is calling you." Heeding their summons, he followed them up into the heavens, wondrous things there to behold.

Long after the boy had become a great holy man of his tribe, Black Elk *(left, in his eighties)* recounted the vision that transformed his life. In it he was shown the great beauty and harmony that pervade the universe, and from the spiritual beings who summoned him, he learned of the sacred symbols and objects that gave the power to heal sickness and quell strife, a gift that would serve his people well in the troubled years ahead.

Near the end of his vision, Black Elk found himself carried east astride his horse, accompanied by the riders of the four quarters until he was standing on the highest of all mountains, while beneath him stretched the "whole hoop of the world." In a painting done by his lifelong friend, Standing Bear, Black Elk is shown at the center of the earth with a spotted eagle—one of his guides—on his shoulder, a sacred flowering stick, and a peace pipe offering smoke to the heavens.

The rapt audience responded to the news with murmurs of thanks to Wakan Tanka. After the youth had completed his report, the holy man passed him the pipe to smoke and then summed up the lessons that could be drawn from the quest. The four colors of the morning star, he explained, represented the four stages of life—infancy, youth, adulthood, and old age—through which all creatures must pass in their journey from birth to death. The message from the woodpecker meant that the young man should always remember Wakan Tanka as he walked the path of life and be attentive to the signs that the Great Mystery had vouchsafed to humanity. Only thus would he grow in wisdom.

The holy man concluded by thanking Wakan Tanka: "You have established a relationship with this young man; and through this relationship he will bring strength to his people. We who are now sitting here represent all the people, and thus we all give thanks to you, O Wakan Tanka. We all raise our hands to you and say, 'Wakan Tanka, we thank you for this understanding and relationship that you have given to us.' Be merciful to us always! May this relationship exist until the very end!" And so the young man was received into the spiritual life of the community.

The vision quest has long been the focal point of the religious life of most Native Americans. The wigwam dwellers of the eastern woodlands, the buffalo hunters of the Great Plains, the salmon fishers of the Pacific Coast, the igloo makers of the frozen north, all shared an extraordinarily direct faith in which each individual established, through dreams and visions, a personal link with the spirit world. Only in the settled agricultural communities of the South and Southwest did the individual religious revelation take second place to the elaborate and complex ceremonial traditions of the group.

Visions provide access to power, the current of supernatural force that courses beneath the surface of every aspect of Indian life. The Abenaki have a saying: "The Great Spirit is in all things; he is in the air we breathe." A Teton Sioux expressed the same thought in a different way: "It is the general belief of the Indians that after a man dies, his spirit is somewhere on the earth or in the sky, we do not know exactly where, but we believe that his spirit still lives. So it is with Wakan Tanka. We believe that he is everywhere, yet he is to us as the spirits of our friends whose voices we cannot hear."

Even so, some places and objects are more highly charged with pow-

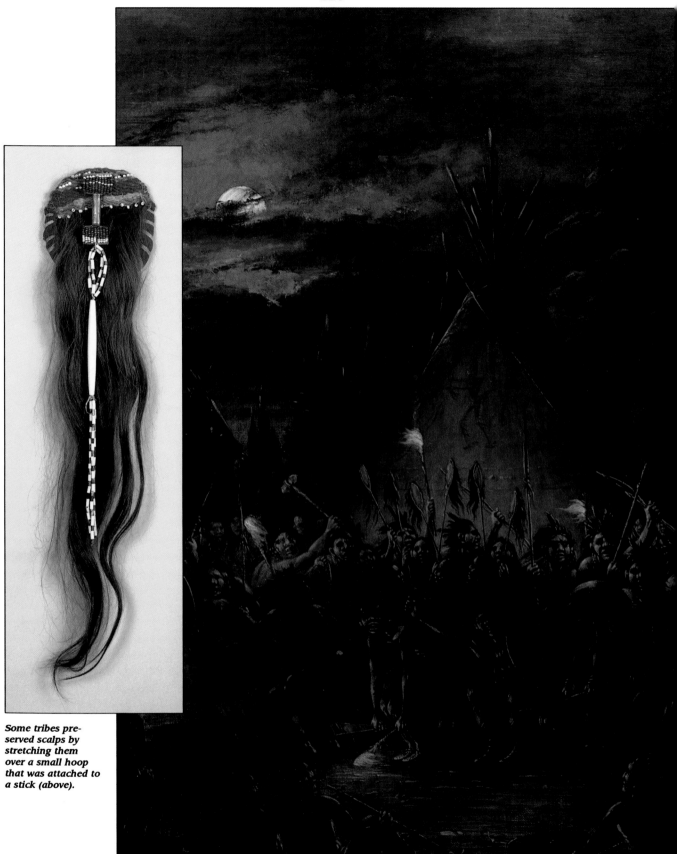

Some tribes preserved scalps by stretching them over a small hoop that was attached to a stick (above).

Sioux warriors dance around the scalps of their foes in an elaborate reenactment of a successful battle. Native Americans believed that hair was a manifestation of life. By taking an enemy's scalp, a warrior also laid claim to his life force, a power that could be used afterward to the victor's advantage.

er than others. Although all power springs from the Great Spirit, it manifests itself in different ways; from great elemental forces like the sun, the moon, and the winds to individual rocks, animals, and trees. Mountaintops are also full of power and so are places near water. Conversely, other spots are especially dangerous—particularly grave sites, where malevolent spirits of the dead may lurk. If the spirits are not appeased by correct behavior, their power can cause harm.

A solitary vision quest, however, is by no means the only route to power. Indians also seek visions through participation in group ceremonies such as the Sun Dance, the great summer ritual of the Plains Indians. And sometimes the visions come unbidden, through the medium of dreams. Several Indian communities put particular emphasis on this channel to the supernatural, among them the Mohave, who live in Arizona and California, and the Iroquois of New York State, of whom a Jesuit missionary noted 300 years ago: "They consider the dream as the master of their lives. It is the God of the country. It is this that dictates to them their feasts, their hunting, their fishing, their war, their trade with the French, their remedies, their dances, their games, their songs."

Women could dream themselves power, which could be used in such traditionally female fields as treating sick children, preparing food, or gathering plants. As a rule, however, strong taboos kept them from participating in male activities. A woman's unique power of giving life was considered antithetic to a man's power to hunt and kill. In traditional tribal days, girls were sequestered in small huts at the time of their first menstruation, typically for a period of 4 to 10 days—a rite that paralleled the adolescent male's vision quest. Thereafter, throughout her childbearing years, a woman had to be rigorously segregated from everything related to hunting. Many Indians believed that should a menstruating woman so much as cross a deer trail, the deer might leave the area.

For boys, however, preparations for the vision quest often began well before puberty. In some communities, children as young as seven or eight were denied food for a day to accustom them to fasting; as they grew older, they would train themselves to endure longer periods. In the meantime, their fathers and grandfathers talked to them about visions in order to prepare them for the experience. In doing so, the boys learned ancestral lore, with the result that members of each Indian community have tended to share similar visions.

When the time for the quest was approaching, the vision seeker, or else a relative who wished to share in the ordeal, would sometimes agree to have many tiny pieces of flesh cut from his arm. The skin was then put inside a rattle for the quester to take with him to shake as he prayed.

Before setting out, the vision seeker had to undergo ritual purification by bathing in a sweat lodge. These tiny, airtight huts, made by covering a circular frame of bent saplings with hides, tarpaulins, or blankets, are familiar to almost every Indian community in North America. They were used not just to prepare for vision quests but also before important ceremonies, raids, or hunting expeditions—as well as for therapy for a variety of ailments, and sometimes just to relax and get clean.

The sweat lodges operate on the principle of a sauna. Helpers working outside the hut heat stones and pass them to the participants inside who pour water over them to make steam. After a time, the entrance flap is lifted to release some of the heat. More stones are provided, and the process begins again. The heat and the heavy perspiration contribute to a sense of transformation, and the participants leave the lodge feeling cleansed in body and spirit.

The details of the quest vary from tribe to tribe. Some Sioux visionaries entombed themselves in pits several feet deep; the opening was then covered with hides and overlaid lightly with earth, to allow air but no light to penetrate to the lonely figure below. More typical was the open-air site with the five wooden poles. Often the prescribed length of time was four days—a sacred number for many Indians—but the quest could be shortened if a vision came earlier.

There was no guaranteeing that a vision would come. In such cases, some determined questers even resorted to self-mutilation; to persuade the spirits to take pity on them, they might cut off a finger joint as an offering. In spite of all that, unsuccessful quests were not uncommon. Then, the disappointed vision seeker simply had to try again, persisting until he was rewarded, for as the Ojibwa saying had it: "No man begins to be until he has seen his vision."

When visions did come, they arrived in various forms, sharing little more than a dreamlike quality and a sense of spiritual authority that stamped them indelibly on the dreamer's mind. Whatever a man saw became his emblem for life. If he dreamed of a specific bird or animal, female relatives might weave its paw, a bit of its skin, or some of its feathers or claws into his possessions. The warrior might also paint a likeness of the creature onto his ritual equipment, such as his pipes and rattles, and even onto his body—just as the Sioux leader Crazy Horse painted himself a flash of lightning on his cheek and patterns of hailstones on his

THE DIVINE PROTECTION OF A WARRIOR'S SHIELD

From ancient times through the present day, Indian peoples of the Southwest and Great Plains have prized shields for their mystic strength. A good shield, traditionally made with the assistance of a shaman, was believed capable of affording the bearer the protection of the gods.

The leather shields frequently bore sacred feathers or symbolic pictures of animals that were painted either on the shield itself or on a buckskin cover. These designs, which customarily had appeared to the owner during a vision, were thought to endow him with the qualities of the animals that were depicted. The medicine power derived not only from the painted symbols, however.

Every step in the carefully defined process of crafting the shield imbued the weapon with additional significance.

As a means of deflecting arrows, lances, and axes, shields had served for generations as effective defensive armor in Native American warfare. But bullets were an entirely different matter. The introduction of firearms by the Europeans rendered the prized shields practically worthless in terms of actual physical protection. Nevertheless, for a long while after rifles became the predominant weapon in the Indians' land, Native Americans continued to believe in the spiritual potency of the shields and still use them today during dance and medicine ceremonies.

Fool Bull, a Sioux medicine man, proudly displays the shield he carried during the Battle of the Little Bighorn, where Custer met legendary defeat.

CRAFTING THE SHIELD

A circle on the buffalo indicates areas on the hump and under the neck from which the toughest hide was taken for shields.

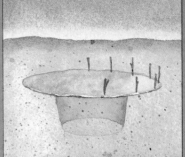

The rawhide was fastened to the ground by means of wooden stakes over a hole that measured approximately 18 inches deep.

One edge of the hide, left un-staked, was raised from time to time, and red-hot stones were dropped into the hole.

The Crow shield below is painted with concentric red circles representing sun halos, the circles seen around the sun when a storm is coming. The black dashes are pieces of a man so little his enemies cannot touch him.

Water was poured onto the rocks until the steam heat generated caused the hide to shrink to half its original size.

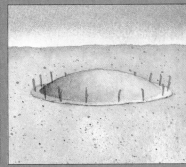

The soft hide was pegged down over a heap of earth, giving the shield a convex shape that increased its deflective powers.

After the shield had been given sufficient time to dry and harden, the craftsmen decorated the disk with pertinent symbols.

A shield belonging to the Crow Chief Arapoosh bears a human image of the moon, which appeared to him in a vision. Shields were often used to predict success. Good fortune would ensue if, when rolled along the ground, they landed faceup. Their landing facedown, however, foretold disaster.

This Hunkpapa Sioux rawhide dance shield is adorned with feathers and symbols of birds, hoofs, a rainbow, and the head of a buffalo. The shields of Plains Indians often displayed feathers and bird imagery, which could impart everything from courage to swiftness to sharp night vision.

A Cheyenne deerskin shield cover is decorated with feathers and the image of a sacred green turtle, which according to Cheyenne tradition supports the earth on its back. A cover like this was not removed from the shield during combat because its design was thought to be powerful medicine that would protect the warrior from harm.

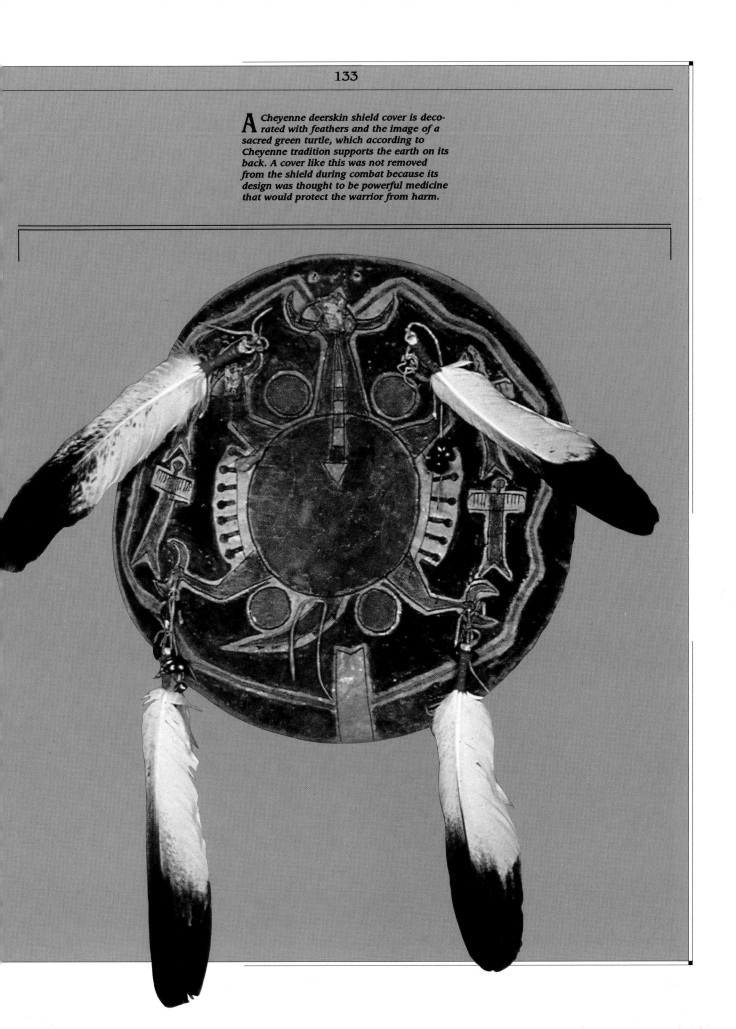

body. The objects seen in a vision also formed the contents of an Indian's medicine bundle, the portable collection of holy things that he carried to renew his spiritual power.

Among the Sioux, the animal spirit seen in a vision determined a man's social affiliation. Each of the various Lakota bands had societies of elk dreamers, buffalo dreamers, deer dreamers, and bear dreamers with membership restricted to individuals who had seen the same creature in their dreams. Furthermore, it was only after successfully completing a vision quest that an Indian received his adult name. Names carried power and could not be bestowed on a young man who had not reached spiritual maturity.

Although nearly all male Indians sought visions, some were more strongly attracted to the world of the spirits than others. These men, who might go on several vision quests during their lifetimes, acquired many guardian spirits. The rest of the community respected and feared them for their special power. These people were the shamans or medicine men. Although the two terms are applied interchangeably, each one of them highlights a different facet of the visionary's powers: *medicine man* stresses the healing role, while *shaman* emphasizes mystic attributes.

Sometimes the two roles were combined. The arctic peoples traditionally believe that humans fall ill because they have lost their souls—either to hostile sorcerers or to bad dreams. Indeed, the notion that the

The Pawnee version of the universe shows stars, including the morning star (top, center), that figured in their creation stories and ceremonies. The Skidi branch used the chart long ago as a type of altar.

soul wandered off during sleep has led some Native Americans to claim that it is possible to kill people by waking them up too suddenly. To effect a cure, shamans would go into trances in which they set off mentally in search of the missing spirit. At times, the shaman had himself tied up with ropes for fear that he might be physically carried away.

In all Indian societies, shamans were expected to put their powers to use for the good of the community. Besides healing, they might be asked to foretell future events, recover lost objects, cast love spells, communicate with the spirits of departed relatives, or bring good weather. Among the Sioux, they had a leadership role in organizing hunting expeditions and war parties; it was they who directed the warriors in search of game or foe, although once the target was sighted, other tribal leaders took command. Such responsibilities could be daunting; if a warrior was killed on a raid or a hunt that had been judged propitious, the community might blame the shaman and in some cases might even sentence him to death.

People were willing to pay large fees, in horses, blankets, or other goods, to secure the services of a respected shaman. To increase their standing, shamans sometimes performed sleight-of-hand displays, made themselves disappear, or had themselves trussed up only to escape, Houdini-like, from their bonds. Among the Crow Indians, shamans staged public contests before large audiences, in the course of which they would make food appear and hand it to their opponents or else employ various tricks to make the audience sway or fall over.

Other shamans were contemptuous of such displays. As one holy man complained to an outsider: "In our forefathers' day, the shamans were solitary men, but now they are all priests or doctors, weather prophets or conjurers producing game, or clever merchants selling their skills for pay." Another spoke of the pain and loneliness that one must endure in order to acquire knowledge. "True wisdom," he said, "is only to be found far away from people, out in the great solitude, and it is not found in play but only through suffering. Solitude and suffering open the human mind, and therefore a shaman seeks his wisdom there."

The shaman's most important public function was healing, a process that could take several different forms according to the type of ailment to be treated. Injuries with obvious causes such as dislocations, fractures, or snake-

Saplings make up the frame for a Chippewa shaking tent, the setting for a shaman's divinations. When the holy man entered and lowered the canvas cover (here blown by the wind), he thought himself to be at the center of the universe where he could make contact with the horizontal world of humans and the vertical world of spiritual beings.

bites were approached in a common-sense way, and treatment was often effective. Internal diseases with no obvious explanation were attributed to supernatural influences. Wasting diseases that involved weakening and the loss of consciousness might be attributed to soul loss, but other aches and infections were more likely to be blamed on a disturbance in the spiritual harmony of the community. Such discord could spring from the breaking of taboos, from the activities of hostile sorcerers, or for the Iroquois at least, from unfulfilled dreams and desires.

Unlike the healers who used herbal medicines to treat the sick, employing little ritual in the process, the shamans' principal medical skills were psychic. The specialty of the most respected medicine men lay in using their power to "see" with the mind's eye the cause of a patient's ailment. Many Native Americans believed that disease took a physical form in the shape of a small pathogen—a ball of fluff, a pebble, a feather—lodged inside the patient's body. The task of the shaman was to locate the pathogen and remove it.

To effect a cure, the shaman needed to call on all his spiritual powers. He would prepare himself by praying and fasting. The exact form of treatment varied from people to people and shaman to shaman. Iroquois medicine men, for instance, used to sip herbal tea and chant invocations to the spirits; then they breathed over the sick person to make the patient's body magically transparent. Alternatively, if sorcery was suspected, they might try to interpret the patient's dreams so as to find the identity of the wrongdoer; or else they might hide their heads under a blanket until the cause of the malady was revealed to them.

A typical Sioux healing session lasted several hours. The medicine man would enter the tipi of the sick person carrying his objects of power—including, perhaps, a pipe, a cup of water, a drum, one or several curing herbs, a bunch of deer hoofs on rawhide to serve as a rattle, and a bone whistle. Beating the drum, he would invoke Wakan Tanka and chant the messages he had learned in his visions. These songs—generally slow and sung to an irregular beat—were regarded as the source of much of his healing power.

While the medicine man sang, he would stroke the patient's body with his hands or wave a stick or feather credited with power. He might blow smoke from the pipe over the diseased limbs. Throughout the treatment, the healer would repeatedly stress his past successes, and would reiterate the claim that the patient was going to be healed, thereby employing the force of affirmative thinking to the process. As the hours

TOOLS OF THE SHAMAN'S TRADE

Even though every Indian shaman possessed a potent set of tools that he employed for healing, nowhere were these sets more elaborate than among the prosperous tribes residing in the Pacific Northwest. One particularly powerful Tlingit shaman was discovered buried near Dry Bay, Alaska, along with no fewer than 45 instruments, including 8 masks, 4 rattles, 3 batons, 3 necklaces, and an amulet of spruce root and ermine skins. Each one of these objects had been carved or painted with an assortment of supernatural powers known as *yek;* these were the spirit helpers of the shaman who had appeared to him during his initiatory vision. So powerful was the shaman's kit that it was never allowed inside a house, except during a curing ceremony. Tradition required that it be stored out-of-doors, often in a hollow tree deep in the forest. The curing process itself was also sacred and could never be photographed. The picture below is a reenactment of a healing ceremony staged for a photographer in 1889. The shaman holds an oystercatcher rattle and wears a painted wooden headdress of a human face *(inset)* that was adorned with eagle feathers, foxtail, and buckskin.

This Haida shaman's necklace comprises charms that rattled as he danced, creating a rhythmic accompaniment to the healing ritual. The killer whale amulet has the features of a raven, a potent supernatural creature associated with physical transformations.

A soul-catcher charm consists of a carved, hollow bone with abalone inset. Because sickness occurred when the soul left the body, the shaman chanted incantations to trap the elusive spirit in the charm and return it to the patient.

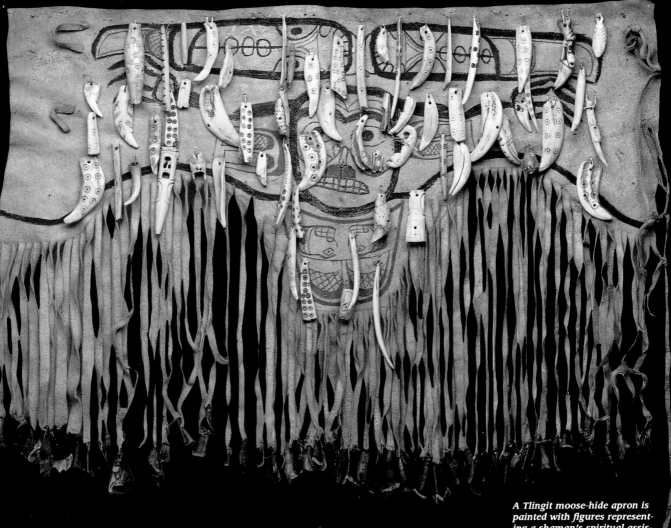

A host of violent spirits populate a shaman's baton (left), including a land otter crushed beneath a disembodied face and a crow with a naked, wide-eyed human in its beak. The shaman used the staff like a spear or club to combat malicious supernatural enemies.

A Tlingit moose-hide apron is painted with figures representing a shaman's spiritual assistants and decorated with ivory and bone charms. The jangling of the charms, along with the deer dewclaws on the fringes, summoned the spirit helpers to aid in the healing

A Tlingit curing amulet made from a bear's canine tooth represents the magical land otter. Some legends say that land otters, which were able to take any form, taught the first shamans the art of transformation.

A shaman reclines on the back of an oystercatcher in this wooden Tlingit shaman's rattle. The oystercatcher, a bird that lives in the boundary between land and ocean, was especially sacred to the shaman.

A crown made of bear claws contributed to the shaman's otherworldly appearance. It also had significant curing powers when rubbed against the body of passed, the songs and chants would slowly rise to a crescendo. Finally, the shaman would apply his lips to the affected part of the body and attempt to suck the pathogen out through the skin. He would then magically produce the object—perhaps a stick, a stone, a worm, or a plant—from his mouth as evidence that a cure had been completed.

The effect on both audience and patient was frequently dynamic. The awe in which the shaman was held, the hypnotic rhythms of drum and rattle, the low, muttered incantation, the dramatic gestures, the final, theatrical moment of success—all could come together to improve the condition of anyone whose disease was susceptible to the power of encouragement. Even medicine men who have admitted that the miraculous appearance of the pathogen was in fact achieved by trickery have insisted that this in no way invalidated the therapy. ''We could cure without that just by singing and remembering the vision,'' a shaman claimed, ''but people need something to see.''

In some communities, patients have been treated in ceremonies that stretch over many days. Navajo rituals, for example, can last from one to nine days, and feature the so-called sand paintings that have become famous among non-Indians for their beauty—although the people who create them are concerned only with their spiritual efficacy. The healer, known as the *ha'athali,* or singer, and as many as 12 assistants gather together in the patient's hogan, the traditional dwelling of the Navajo, to create the painting. The healers dribble grains of ground sandstone through their fingertips onto the floor. The images they create summon the supernatural beings to enter into the curing process.

When the designs are completed, the singer sprinkles them with pollen and places objects from his medicine bundle around them. Then, the patient enters the hogan and is ritually bathed, dried with cornmeal, and painted with symbols of the spirits. As a last step in the preparation process, a turquoise stone is tied in his or her hair. The patient then sits on the painting to become a part of it, thus uniting with the spirits. The healing powers of the spirits course through the patient's limbs, bringing about the cure. Afterward, the sand is swept up and scattered to the four directions, and a final night of prayer and singing follows.

If a shaman's best efforts proved unsuccessful, his only recourse was to blame the disease on a hostile medicine man, or to insist that the taboo violation that originally caused the ailment was so great that it was beyond his power to remedy. He made such admissions unwillingly. Just as repeated successes could bolster a medicine man's reputation and psychologically predispose patients to expect a cure, so a string of failures could destroy a reputation.

The strangest of all Native American medicine men were the contraries, or sacred clowns. These were individuals who had been condemned by the nature of their vision to act in a way that ran counter to normal practice. Among the Sioux, they were known as *heyoka,* and their ranks were made up of men who had dreams of thunderstorms. Black Elk has attempted to explain the connection: "When a vision comes from the thunder beings of the west, it comes with terror like a thunderstorm; but when the storm of vision has passed, the world is greener and happier. The world, you see, is happier after the terror of the storm."

Heyokas swam in icy pools in winter complaining of the heat, pretended to shiver with cold in the hottest days of summer, and faced backward while riding horses. They carried crooked bows and bent arrows, or used bows that were so ridiculously long that they were impossible to shoot. Most spectacular of all, they conducted ceremonies that climaxed with them plunging their arms into cauldrons of boiling water—an ordeal that they prepared for by secretly smearing their arms with chewed leaves of the mallow plant.

The Iroquois equivalent of the heyokas were the Society of False Faces, named after the grotesque masks they wore for their ceremonies. The False Faces received their vocation as a result of visions or dreams. The origins of the society stretch back to two tribal legends. One story tells of a hideous giant who lived at the rim of the world. One day, the giant challenged the benevolent Iroquois Creator to a contest in which each would show off his power by moving a mountain. The giant succeeded in shifting the mountain a certain distance by magic, but the Creator bettered him by bringing the mountain up so close that when the giant turned around to look, he bent his nose against the slopes—an occurrence the Iroquois commemorate through the twisted masks.

The other tale features strange, semihuman beings that the Iroquois used to encounter in the woods. These troublesome spirits would raid the Iroquois camps, pawing through the ashes of the fires in search of scraps of food and tobacco. Though mischievous, they were not dangerous, and they even had healing powers that they were willing to convey to the Indians in exchange for a gift of tobacco.

The Society of False Faces acted out both stories each year at the major Iroquois festivals. Members imitating the forest spirits would run from lodge to lodge emitting eerie cries, entering each dwelling on hands and

A Cayuga Iroquois False Face shakes his turtle-shell rattle to scare away sickness. The gnarled mask represents the disease spirit, whose face was long ago distorted when a rival caused him to smash his nose on a mountain.

knees, and making their way to the fire, which they would extinguish with their bare hands. They would then scatter the ashes around the room, as though searching for tobacco, blowing some of the ashes onto the family members, an action that bestowed health. The family would then beat a stick on a bench and sing while the maskers capered out a dance before running off to the next house. Meanwhile, youngsters, also imitating the forest spirits, would run around the village begging—and sometimes stealing—tobacco and food.

During the great Iroquois Midwinter Festival, the False Faces provided comic relief by bursting into the tribal council house to perform an awkward dance dedicated to the giant that opposed the Creator. In spite of all their clownish behavior, however, the False Faces were frequently consulted as healers. They treated toothaches, nosebleeds, and earaches, as well as ailments of the head, shoulders, and joints.

The extraordinary prestige accorded to successful shamans often gave them leadership positions with influence that extended to neighboring tribes. As European penetration of North America gathered pace, a succession of charismatic medicine men tried to rally Indian resistance by reasserting the old certainties of their people's culture. Called prophets by the Europeans, these shamans warned of the dangers of deserting the traditional ways. In 1762, Neolin, a Delaware holy man, traveled among the Indian communities along the banks of Lake Erie, calling the people back to their ancient beliefs. The preachings of Neolin prepared the way for the war leader Pontiac to organize a great intertribal confederacy to confront the white settlers. At the end of the 18th century, Handsome Lake, a Seneca medicine man with a history of alcoholism emerged from a near-death experience with a similar message. He called it *Gaiwiio,* or Good Word; it claims several thousand adherents to this day. In the mid-19th century, a Wanapum shaman named Smohalla formed a group known as the Dreamers who led resistance to the government's attempts to turn the Indians of the Northwest into farmers, a way of life that they considered harmful to nature. "You ask me to plow the ground," he would tell government agents. "Shall I take a knife and tear my mother's bosom? Then when I die, she will not take me to her bosom to rest."

Moving in a slow, shuffling circle, four Arapaho women perform the Ghost Dance in 1893. The purpose of this widely popular dance was to bring about the disappearance of the white man and the return of ancestral lands to the Indians.

The most widespread of all the prophetic movements was originated in 1869 by a Paiute medicine man named Wodziwob. He had a vision that the transcontinental railroad, which had just been completed, would bring recently deceased tribesmen back from the dead, a miracle that would be the sign for a general revival in the fortunes of the Native American peoples. In the meantime, the Paiute were to prepare themselves by reviving a traditional Round Dance that symbolically repeated the sun's journey across the sky. Wodziwob's vision attracted a great deal of attention, but it lost support when the hoped-for train failed to arrive. Instead, a drought came to further deplete the Paiute's dwindling resources and destroy Wodziwob's credibility.

During the following two decades, the plight of Indians throughout the West deteriorated rapidly. A wave of white settlers followed the railroad, impinging on the Indian lands. As the whites slaughtered the last of

Stars painted on an Arapaho Ghost Dance shirt symbolize hope for the coming of a new age for the Indian. The turtle is a symbol of the spirit world, while the magpies and crows represent the belief that Ghost Dancers would be flown out of danger when the next world dawned. Many dancers felt that a Ghost Dance shirt would protect the wearer from all harm, including bullets.

the buffalo on the Great Plains, a sense of despair spread through tribes that had seen their old lifestyles overwhelmed. With their traditional beliefs seemingly powerless to intervene, the mood among the Indians was ripe for a new message of hope.

Its bearer was a fellow tribesman of Wodziwob named Wovoka, who lived in the Mason Valley of western Nevada. In his youth, Wovoka had worked for a Presbyterian rancher who introduced him to Christianity and gave him the name of Jack Wilson. Wovoka revived the message of his predecessor on the strength of a vision he experienced while deliriously ill during an eclipse of the sun on January 1, 1889. In Wovoka's own words, "When the sun died, I went up to heaven and saw God and all the people who had died a long time ago. God told me to come back and tell my people they must be good and love one another, and not fight, or steal, or lie. He gave me this dance to give my people." Because it was expected to help raise the dead, the ritual that he promoted soon became known as the Ghost Dance.

Wovoka's message was apocalyptic. The existing world was coming to an end. It would be destroyed by a great flood. The spirits of Indians both dead and alive would then inhabit a new world to which they would fly through the air with the aid of magic feathers. There they would live as they had before the coming of the white man. To prepare themselves for the great day, Indians must live correctly and above all must gather regularly to practice the Ghost Dance.

Word of the new prophet—described by some whites as the "Indian who impersonated Christ"—raced like wildfire through the dispirited Native American communities of the West. Soon Indian groups from southern California to Oklahoma and the Dakotas were practicing the dance. Forming in a great circle, the participants moved clockwise in the direction of the sun with slow, shuffling steps around a central fire. All the while, they sang special Ghost Dance songs. In the emotionally charged atmosphere of the dance, it was common for individual dancers to suddenly collapse in a trance. On awakening, they would recount the visions they had seen and spontaneously compose songs about them to add to the Ghost Dance repertoire.

Although Wovoka's own message was peaceful, it became distorted as it spread by word of mouth to other tribes. On the Great Plains, the spiritual revival took a warlike turn. There, hunger and hardship were compounded by indignation over the government's campaign to bully the Sioux into selling large portions of their common reservation. In their despair, they interpreted Wovoka's vision to mean that the slaughtered herds of buffalo would return to the prairies and that the white settlers would be swept away. Large numbers of Sioux began gathering for Ghost Dance sessions, many dressed in shirts painted with images derived from visions. The images were believed to make the garment bulletproof. Fearing an uprising, nervous Indian agents called in federal troops. While soldiers were attempting to disarm a group of Sioux at Wounded Knee, South Dakota, one icy morning at the end of 1890, a shot rang out. In the ensuing melee, the U.S. 7th Cavalry Regiment, Custer's old unit, slaughtered up to 300 Indians, many of them women and children.

The Wounded Knee massacre put an end to the Ghost Dance in Sioux territory. Elsewhere, the dance continued to be performed for several more years, with declining enthusiasm as the promised millennium failed to materialize. Although the movement died out, Wovoka, its prophet, remained a respected and powerful shaman until his death in 1932.

The shamans of many tribes grouped together into so-called medicine societies in much the same way that Indians of a military bent formed warrior societies. Such clans were particularly popular among the settled, agricultural peoples of the Southwest; the Zuni of New Mexico, for example, have at least 13 different societies, each one of them tracing its origin back to a vision experienced by its founder and possessing its own songs and ceremonies that have been passed down from generation to generation.

The most celebrated of all medicine societies was the Midewiwin—a word thought to derive from words meaning "good-hearted"—of the tribes in the Great Lakes region. Its rituals were kept secret from nonmembers, and joining entailed a long, arduous process. A new recruit would first be instructed in herbal lore and in the traditions of the society.

Masked Koyemshi clowns tramp through Zuni Pueblo. Teaching by bad example, these contraries exaggerate vice and other antisocial practices, mocking all that is held sacred and lampooning greed and gluttony by stuffing themselves with food during rituals.

If he proved a satisfactory candidate, he would be admitted to the first grade of membership and be expected to contribute a membership fee, payable in skins and foodstuffs. He then underwent an elaborate initiation ceremony that climaxed when a white shell was pointed at his chest. The shell was the most treasured possession of the society and symbolic of one in tribal legend that appeared out of the sea to lead the tribe to their homeland. At this point, the initiate would at once fall down as though dead, supposedly shot by the powerful shell, only to be revived by his colleagues as a member of the society.

Similar rituals accompanied the novice's subsequent progress through the three superior grades, each of which implied a higher degree of spiritual power. By the time he had been admitted to the fourth order, he was a full-fledged shaman.

Besides the elaborate rituals of the medicine societies, shamans also played a leading role in the public ceremonies that were an essential part of tribal life. Each community had its own traditional rites, hallowed by time and honored by annual repetition. Ceremonial life was especially well developed among the Pueblos, whose every community supported a whole corps of ritual officiants. But even the nomadic Plains peoples had regular annual gatherings for which the whole population would assemble. These meetings provided opportunities to trade, exchange information, visit relatives, gossip, even find possible marriage partners. They also reaffirmed the group's cultural identity and renewed its relationship with the spirit world.

Ritual has always been an instinctive Indian response to the sacred aspects of everyday life. Small ceremonial gestures accompany even the most routine activities. Traditionally, a Sioux when eating will always set aside a morsel for the spirits of departed friends. Hunters had to sing special songs before setting off in search of prey, and then had to bury the bones of animals they killed in the proper manner to ensure a continued supply of game. Individuals might have their own private rites, too. In the 1960s, an Assiniboin from Montana described his father's habits thus: "He never neglected his thanks early in the morning when he'd be out and the sun came up, shining—that's the eye of the Great Spirit. When the sun got about there, noon, he stopped, just for a few seconds, gave thanks to the

Great Spirit and asked to be blessed. Then again when the sun was going down, he watched that until it got out of sight."

Communal celebrations often coincide with notable natural events, such as the winter or summer solstice or the spring or autumn equinox. Rituals also mark milestones in an individual's life, such as birth, naming, or marriage. The Ojibwa celebrated a young hunter's first kill, the onset of womanhood in an adolescent—commemorated on her return from menstrual sequestration—and an annual Feast of the Dead, which memorialized all

members of the tribe who had died the previous year. The Pueblo ceremonial calendar is a constant round of public and private events, some marked by the appearance of the masked and costumed kachina dancers representing spirits of rain and fertility.

The purpose of the ceremonies is not so much to worship the spirits as to show them respect as fellow residents of the universe. As such, they need propitiation more than reverence. To win their approval, each ceremony must be repeated in exact detail year after year. Yet few tribes have ever been so conservative in their habits that they would not borrow new rituals from neighbors or even enemies if they were reputed to be effective.

Although the ceremonies are infinitely varied in detail, they typically involve dancing to the chanting of sacred songs, the shaking of rattles, the blowing of whistles, and the hypnotic rhythms of the drums. Black Elk once explained the drum's symbolic importance: "Its round form represents the universe, and its steady strong beat is the pulse, the heart, throbbing at the center of the universe. As the voice of Wakan Tanka, it stirs and helps us to understand the mystery and the power of things."

In many communities, the solemnity of the ceremonies has been relieved traditionally by the antics of the sacred clowns, who mock the shamans, lampoon the dancers, and interrupt the proceedings by shouting gibberish. Among the Zuni, the clowns even parrot the most holy prayers, substituting obscene phrases for the originals. Navajo clowns make fun of the sleight-of-hand tricks practiced by the shamans, clumsily revealing their secrets. Besides providing comic relief, the foolery supplies an important counterweight to the seriousness of the rest of the ritual—an essential aspect in the Indian world, where all things must be in balance.

One feature notable by its scarcity in Native American ceremonial life is the notion of sacrifice. Although many tribes killed enemy prisoners as a matter of course, there is nothing to compare with the practices of the ancient Aztecs of Central America who, in their prime, may have performed as many as 10,000 human sacrifices a year.

One of the few authenticated examples of human sacrifice in North America is the Morning Star Ceremony of the Pawnee of Nebraska, which was practiced well into the 19th century. In years when Mars rose in the east, the tribe would sometimes sacrifice a girl snatched expressly for

Standing in the fork of the Sun Pole and blowing a bone whistle, a Kootenay chief leads members of his tribe in raising a sun dance lodge at Hot Springs, Montana, in the summer of 1914 (far left). In a different version of the dance, Oglala Teton Sioux celebrants placed a bleached and painted buffalo skull (left) in the fork of the Sun Pole on the fifth day of the ceremony. While the lodge symbolized the earth or man's home, the buffalo skull represented the spiritual essence of life.

that purpose from a neighboring people's village. The aim was to propitiate the planet, which would appear in human form to a tribesman in a vision, directing him to find a suitable victim.

For three days after her capture, the girl was well treated while the Pawnee performed preparatory ceremonies directed by the morning star priest, the only person in the community who knew the full ritual. The climax of the ceremony began after midnight on the fourth day. The priest led the people in singing and dancing through the long hours of the night. Just before dawn, the girl was brought out naked, her body painted half red and half black. She had been kept in ignorance of her fate, for it was considered important that she voluntarily mount the scaffold that had been set up in the middle of the camp. Once she had mounted its rungs, she was tied spread-eagled, her face toward the morning star. Suddenly, a warrior ran up to her, clutching a flaming brand with which he made as if to touch her under the arms and on the genitals, but pulling the fire back at the last moment. Then another warrior appeared, and shot an arrow through the girl's heart.

At once a priest cut her breast with a flint knife, smearing blood from the cut onto his face. Others ran up with dried buffalo meat, which was also anointed with blood and placed on the fire as an offering. Then the entire community shot arrows into the lifeless corpse, shouting and dancing as they did so. Mothers even fired arrows on behalf of their infants, for it was important that the whole community be associated with the killing. Then the body was taken out of the village and left to become one with the earth, while the tribe gave itself up to celebration and feasting.

A painted Ute deer hide from the 1890s depicts both the Sun Dance with its lodge of poles and beneath it a performance of the Bear Dance. While the Sun Dance reaffirmed the tribe's connections with supernatural forces, the Bear Dance celebrated the coming of spring and the bears' awakening from hibernation.

Clutching his favorite bow and a medicine bundle, a Sioux warrior leans back in agony against rawhide restraints that pass from the Sun Pole to skewers pushed under the skin of his chest as part of the Sun Dance. George Catlin, who painted the scene above, witnessed one man's ordeal. "With the blood trickling down over his body, which was covered with white and yellow clay, and amidst a large crowd who were looking on and encouraging him, he was 'looking at the sun' without paying the least attention to anyone about him," he explained.

In the early 1800s, about the time that the Morning Star Ceremony was dying out, a new ritual gained popularity among the peoples of the Great Plains. Called the Sun Dance by the Sioux, it was derived from the ancient ceremonials of many different tribes and it soon became the focal religious event of nearly all the Indian peoples west of the Missouri River. If any single event could be said to bring together all the strands of Native American spirituality, it was this elaborate ceremony featuring prolonged self-denial as well as physical pain on an extraordinary scale.

The emergence of the Sun Dance came in the heyday of the Plains Indians. They had entered a golden age in the 18th century, when groups that had previously existed precariously from hunting and gathering or small-scale agriculture acquired horses in large numbers, originally from Spanish settlers in what is now New Mexico. The huge herds of buffalo that roamed the grasslands could now be hunted with vastly greater efficiency. The enhanced meat supply made it possible for massive tribal assemblies to come together each summer for the hunt. The Sun Dance became the focus of these gatherings for nearly all of the tribes that migrated to the Plains.

The dance achieved its greatest complexity among the Arapaho, Cheyenne, and Sioux, and it was from the latter's habit of gazing at the sun as they danced that it was to take its name. The appellation was slightly misleading, since for most of the peoples who performed the dance, the sun was not the main focus of attention. Rather, the ceremony was an annual opportunity to affirm the unity of the tribe and to reestablish its relationship with the supernatural powers, which had brought forth plenty in the past and, if duly respected, would do so again.

The general outline of the Sun Dance was similar for every tribe. To get it under way, a patron had to be found to sponsor the building of a sun dance lodge and the feasts associated with the gathering. This was a serious commitment that involved not only great expense but also long periods of fasting and praying. It was usually undertaken by someone who had recently lost a loved one and who wanted to make the sacrifices involved in memory of the departed.

In the ensuing months, word went out about the time and location of the ceremony, which would be publicly consecrated with buffalo hunts that also served to provide food for the feasts that followed the dancing. The shaman responsible for the tribe's sun dance bundle took charge of organizing the event. He spent a great deal of time in the weeks preceding the ceremony with the sponsor, sharing his spiritual travails as well as working out practical details of the celebrations.

The entire ceremony normally lasted more than eight days. Building the special camp dominated the activities of the first four days. The camp's focal point was a center pole, the Sun Pole, and elaborate rituals accompanied its raising. Once a suitable tree was found, the Indians treated it like a human enemy; the entire camp rode out to count coup on the tree, striking it with the ritual gesture usually reserved for enemy warriors. When the tree was finally cut down and stripped of its bark, a fork was left at its top so that a buffalo skull and other medicine objects could be hung there during the ceremony.

From the moment the tree was felled, all participants began a fast that would end only when the dance was over three or four days later. The pole was raised as the center point of the circular camp, ringed by the tipis of the assembled tribe and by a circular awning constructed from saplings and branches to provide shade for the spectators. Once the structures were all in place, the dance began.

On the eve of the match, each side holds a dance for victory. In the photograph at right, seven women, representing the seven Cherokee clans, dance and chant to the beat of the seated drummer, while the players, holding their sticks, circle a sacred fire.

Wearing the traditional breechcloth and eagle feathers, a Cherokee player stoically submits to the ritual scratching by a shaman that precedes a game. Considered a charm, the marks are made in groups of four and seven, numbers sacred to the tribe.

A GAME PLAYED FOR THE GODS

"Almost everything short of murder" is how one observer described the tactics of Cherokee ballplayers as they battled furiously with sticks, punches, and tackles to score. But despite the fierce rivalry and frequent injuries, this game, akin to lacrosse, has always been much more than a simple athletic contest. As with other Indian games, it is primarily a sacred ritual, a reenactment of the constant struggle between the opposing forces of the universe. Like the Cherokee deities, the Twin War Gods, the ballplayers duel determinedly as part of the natural order, the netted pockets of their sticks inspired by the spider-web shields of the divine twins. For several weeks before a game, the players practice their skills, avoiding contact with women and children, while shamans exhort them to victory and call on supernatural powers to give them swiftness and strength.

Near Peach Springs, Arizona, a Walapai cry shed, a memorial to the dead, catches fire at daybreak. Periodically, the Walapai build such a structure and fill it with pictures and mementos of dead relatives, as well as with symbolic belongings that may be of use in the next world. The smoke of the fire carries the blessing to the souls of the departed.

Drums pounded and whistles shrieked. The dancers remained in place, raising themselves up and down on their toes while gazing in the general direction of the sun or at the sacred medicine bundle objects adorning the center pole. As the dancing continued into the second and third day, there would be brief interruptions as participants collapsed in exhaustion. Dragged into the shade, they might remain unconscious for several hours. The visions that came to them during that time were rich in power, and new songs, dance steps, and curing techniques were often communicated to them in that way.

However great the suffering of the ordinary Sun Dancers, it paled beside the ordeal of those individuals who had made vows to submit themselves to self-torture as a way of winning the sympathy of the spirits or as a means of showing thanks for their good fortune. Usually, the decision to undergo such an ordeal was made during times of stress, perhaps while on the warpath or following the death of a loved one. The covenanter committed himself to having the skin of his chest pierced with a knife so that two wooden skewers could be inserted through the flesh. The ends of buffalo-hide thongs hanging from the top of the Sun Pole were then tied to the skewers. The participant was expected to break loose by hurling himself backward with sufficient force to free the skewers. Alternatively, he might be pierced through the back and attached by thongs to two or more heavy buffalo skulls, which he would then be forced to drag behind him until he broke free.

The self-mutilation so shocked white observers that the United States government banned the Sun Dance from 1904 until 1935. Yet its practitioners have always insisted that it must be understood as a religious rite. "Many white men think of it as an initiation into manhood, or a way to prove one's courage," the Sioux John Lame Deer once explained. "But that is wrong. The Sun Dance is a prayer and a sacrifice."

The Oglala holy man Black Elk stressed the mystic significance of the ordeal. "As we thus break loose," he said, "it is as if we were being freed from the bonds of the flesh."

Once the last bleeding and exhausted dancer was helped to a resting place by admiring friends and relatives, the mood of the gathering relaxed. The Sun Dance came to an end in feasting and gift giving. The Indians had reason to feel contentment. They had played their appointed part in the unending compact with the unseen forces all about them. Now they could go their ways secure in the knowledge that the bond with the spirit world had been renewed. ◆

Smoke rises from the vents of tipis at a Blackfoot camp in this hand-tinted photograph taken around 1900. Dark bands at the top and bottom of the painted tipi (second from left) signify the sky and the earth, while the animal scene in between likely depicts a message from the spirit world that was received by the head of the household during a vision.

THE SACRED SHELTERS

"Beauty extends from the fireside of my hogan," proclaims an old Navajo house-blessing hymn. "Beauty radiates from it in every direction." The beauty celebrated in the song was not physical. Indeed, to outsiders, the earth-covered Navajo hogan might appear plain, even crude. But like other Native American dwellings, the hogan embodied spiritual values that made it luminous to its inhabitants.

The same inner radiance was considered to be a part of shelters as dissimilar as the collapsible hide-covered tipis of the Plains-dwelling Sioux and the imposing cedar lodges of northwestern communities. In these, as in most Indian houses, a central firepit served as the secular and sacred heart of the home, around which family members not only prepared meals but also praised the nourishing spirits. Symbolically, this hearth often represented the navel of the earth, while the smoke hole above it was looked upon as a passageway to the heavens.

The various types of dwellings also served as a metaphor for the world-view of the community. Accordingly, the Iroquois regarded their long houses, each of which sheltered several families, as symbols of the tribal confederacy. The Hidatsa of North Dakota, who lived in four-posted lodges with earthen domes, saw their homes as representations of the celestial vault, which they believed was held aloft by four giant pillars. In a similar manner, other Native American peoples viewed their tipis, kivas, or wigwams as models of their society or of the world. The very act of building them was at the same time a means of comprehending the universe as well as an acceptance of one's place in the cosmic order.

Photographed in 1888, a Haida chief holding a prized sheet of copper stands before a dwelling called The House Where People Always Want to Go. Haida homes have often been given proper names to signify that they have a life of their own. Many houses, like this one, have a ceremonial entryway at the base of the totem pole and a swing door to one side for everyday use.

SANCTUARY BETWEEN FOREST AND SEA

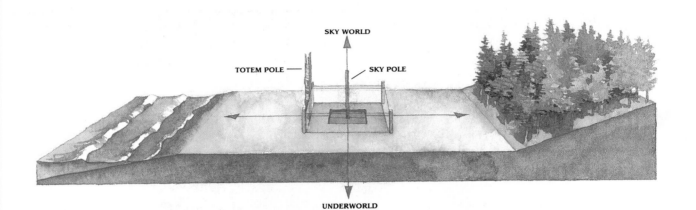

Supernatural pathways—linking the sea to the forest and the underworld to the sky world—intersect at the Haida hearth.

"What instinct, or, rather, what genius, it has required to conceive and execute solidly those edifices, those heavy frames," marveled French explorer Étienne Marchand in 1792, when he arrived at the Queen Charlotte Islands off the coast of British Columbia and beheld the massive plank houses of the Haida Indians. More than 50 feet wide and nearly half again as long, they were built of tightly joined 4-foot-wide cedar planks. Standing side by side, each of them fronted with a towering cedar totem pole carved with crests symbolizing the lineage of its inhabitants, the structures reflected a culture that was rich in material and spiritual resources.

The Haida believed that the universe was divided into three separate zones. The underworld, from which souls emerged at birth, was ruled by the killer whale and associated with the life-giving sea, from which the Haida derived most of their nourishment. The sky world, the realm of the dead, was dominated by the mythical thunderbird and associated with the soaring evergreens of the forest that furnished the timber they used for their houses and canoes. In between the two realms lay the flat disk of the earth, supported on a giant cedar pole that rested on the chest of a supernatural being known as Sacred One Standing and Moving.

Each Haida house represented the center of the universe for the kinship group that inhabited it. Dwellings faced the nurturing sea; the back door looked out on the forest, where the remains of the dead were interred in wooden grave houses. The interior space was clearly defined by status and gender. The front of the dwelling was the domain of low-ranking individuals; the rear was the place of power and reserved ceremonially for the house chief. The left side was associated with the activities of women; the right with the undertakings of men.

The Haida made contact with their ancestral spirits through the smoke hole, honoring the dead with offerings of burnt food. During special ceremonies, a cedar pole—the sky pole—was raised though the smoke hole; a shaman then climbed the pole to dramatize his access to the sky powers.

Inside the house, the floor has been excavated to create a timber-lined central pit for cooking that also served as a site for rituals.

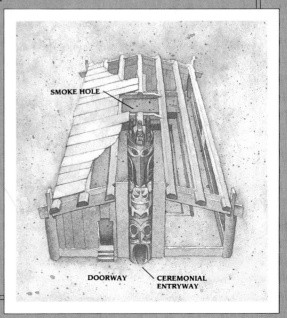

Women of a Navajo family gather at the entrance to their hogan in 1914. After ritually blessing a new hogan, family members would use it as their home and place of worship until an ill omen such as death by disease occurred within; at that point, they would extinguish the fire and abandon the dwelling, known thereafter as a dead hogan, or "no-hearth home."

HOME PLACE DESIGNED IN HEAVEN

The Blessingway, the Navajo tale of creation, relates how a deity named Talking God made a home for First Man and First Woman. Taking as his model a promontory in New Mexico that the Navajo called the "Heart of the Earth" (known today as Gobernador Knob), Talking God built a rounded peak, supported by poles made of white shell, turquoise, abalone, and obsidian. Covered with sunbeams and rainbows, this was the first hogan, or "home place" in the Navajo language.

The earthly incarnations of this mythical shelter include a number of circular, single-roomed structures made of different materials and built in accordance with a variety of plans. The forked-pole hogan that is pictured at left, however, is believed to be the oldest and truest to the fabled form. Its entryway faces east, toward the blessing rays of the rising sun. Three forked, interlocking support poles, which have been planted to the north, west, and south, provide the basic framework of the building. In a symbolic link to the first hogan, small chips of shell, turquoise, and abalone are frequently placed underneath the posts. The frame is filled in with shorter timbers, chinked with narrow strips of wood and bark, and then coated with either mud or earth.

Tradition divides the small interior *(below)*—rarely more than 12 feet in diameter—into male and female sectors, with men keeping their belongings on the south side, and women confining such items as dishes and food to the north side. Movement within the hogan is ritually prescribed: People must make their way around the ceremonial hearth in a sunwise, or clockwise, direction, mimicking the course of the sun as it arcs from east to west across the southern sky.

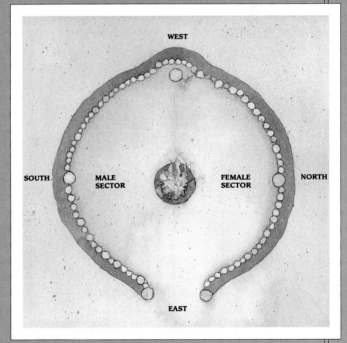

In the typical hogan, three poles support the roof, while two vertical poles frame the eastern entrance (symbolizing the Earth World). The place of honor is at the western end (Water World), which divides the male sector to the south (Mountain World) from the female sector to the north (Corn World).

REFUGE IN A COLD LAND

Inhabitants of the Arctic have for generations gathered under spacious domes for their recreation and rituals. Throughout Inuit territory, villagers fashioned communal structures in a time-honored manner. They dug a pit, built a log framework above it, and covered the structure with an insulating layer of earth, as shown here. Known as a kashim, the house served as a retreat for men as well as a location for village ceremonies.

The snug kashim symbolized and reinforced the solidarity of the circle that met there—a tight band of hunters whose success depended on teamwork. Inside the structure, a central fire kept the chamber so warm that even in the depths of winter, men wore little or no clothing as they ate, traded tales, and repaired their gear on wooden benches along the walls. Married men sometimes spent the night in the kashim, and their unmarried comrades slept there regularly.

Every 7 to 10 days, the men closed the smoke hole, stoked up the fire, and took a sweat bath, breathing through respirators that were woven of grass or shavings to protect their lungs from the smoke

and searing heat. "The men sit naked about the room until they are in profuse perspiration," observed one witness. "They then bathe in urine, which combines with the oil on their bodies, and thus takes the place of soap, after which they go outside and pour water over their bodies."

This cleansing ceremony was just one of the rituals that bound together the members of a hunting clan from about the time that they were 12 years of age, when they first proved strong enough to wield weapons and thereby gained entry to the kashim circle. Once there, they were given the opportunity to absorb the legends and lore of their elders and to join in tests of strength and skill such as wrestling matches.

Access to the kashim was not restricted to the hunters. Women brought meals to their menfolk, initially presenting the platter to animal fetishes on the walls before serving the food. And during an annual winter ceremony, the inflated bladders of slain sea mammals were hung from the ceiling and duly honored by the whole village before they were returned to the ocean to ensure the group's future success in the hunt.

WOVEN GRASS RESPIRATOR

The drafty entryway of the kashim was sealed in wintertime, and villagers passed through a hatchway in the floor in order to reach the interior. Here, as in the Navajo hogan, the place of honor was located opposite the entrance; the space near the door was relegated, in the words of one visitor, to "orphan boys and friendless persons."

Blanketed with earth to conserve heat, the dome-shaped roof of a kashim built early in the 20th century in Nunivak, Alaska, blends inconspicuously into its surroundings. Primarily a house for men, the kashim also accommodated women and children at times of festivity or when visitors arrived; guests were expected to sing and dance in the house and offer presents to their hosts.

ENTRYWAY

SUPPORT POLES

ENTRYWAY

HATCHWAY

FIRE DRAFT

A BIG HOUSE TO HONOR THE CREATOR

The Delaware Indians—who lived along the river of that name before being displaced to Oklahoma—tell of a time long ago when their ancestors grew careless and neglected their time-honored observances. Before long, a great earthquake struck their homeland and shook the ground so terribly that even the animals began to pray. Full of remorse, the Delaware gathered in council to consider what they could do to placate their angry creator. Several men rose to relate an identical vision. Each imparted the same message: "First of all, there must be a house built."

Thus was established the institution of the Delaware Big House, the heart of every community, where countless generations would gather dutifully to praise their maker. Its design obeyed the plan dictated by the Creator in the vision—a long house with a gabled roof and two firepits set beneath smoke holes on either side of a tall center post. The Creator also decreed that the center post be carved with two identical faces "just like mine, painted half black and half red, as mine is, and I will put my power in them." The

carved image shown here also appears on the 10 wall posts. Each of the masks represented 1 of the 12 levels that made up the universe.

The center post of the Big House became the focal point of a rite of thanksgiving that lasted 12 days. To the Delaware, this sacred post represented the World Tree that ascended to heaven from soil deposited on the back of a great turtle to form the earth. Among the three societies that convened in the Big House for the annual rite, the Wolf Clan generally played host and sat at the north end. Two other societies, the Turkey and Turtle clans, sat at the south and west sides, respectively. Periodically, worshipers would rise to sing and dance, circling the center post and firepits. As the days passed, the celebrants could feel themselves drawing closer to the Creator. Then, on the twelfth night, they put on their finery and symbolically entered heaven. The morning after, they returned to earth, prayed a thanksgiving, and again took up their daily tasks, but they remained ever mindful of the Creator's solemn warning: "Never give up the Big House."

Linking earth to sky at the center of the compass, the World Tree served as the axis for the three clans celebrating in the Big House.

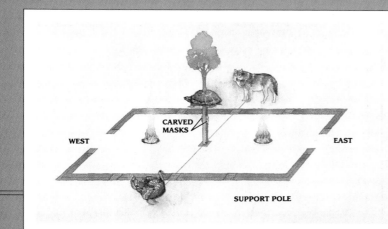

WEST

CARVED MASKS

EAST

SUPPORT POLE

In a 1912 painting of the Big House rite, celebrants circle the firepits and center post, along the so-called White Path symbolizing life's journey.

Prized and preserved by the Delaware Indians despite its fragile condition, this rough-hewn Big House located in northern Oklahoma with its two gaping smoke holes was the site of the last complete thanksgiving ritual held in 1924 by local members of the tribe.

AN EARTHLY LIKENESS OF THE CELESTIAL DOME

Over the flat, unaccented landscape of the Great Plains, the stars shine at night with an enveloping brilliance. To the Pawnee Indians, a seminomadic people centered in Nebraska, this majestic display was nothing less than divine. The shining vault above them was the dome of the lodge that had been built by their heavenly father, the god Tirawahat. And the stars themselves were revered spirits. When the Pawnee died, they entered this heavenly company, traveling through the Milky Way, past the flickering campfires of their departed tribesmen.

The circular lodge inhabited by the still-living Pawnee was covered with a thick layer of earth, but a wide smoke hole in the roof afforded the people inside the dwelling a glimpse of the stars, from which they drew their strength. Four inner support poles reaching from the floor to the ceiling around the firepit were aligned to the northeast, southeast, southwest, and northwest, and painted black, red, white, and yellow, respectively—colors that were associated with star gods who, according to legend, supplied Tirawahat with the invisible posts that hold up their quadrants of the sky vault. The Pawnee lodges were built with the entryway facing to the east so that the inhabitants could see the morning star—the god of light and fire—that would shine on the hearth as a manifestation of the daily miracle of renewal.

Pawnee legend held that each of their villages was founded by a particular star, who told one person how to assemble a bundle of sacred objects related to its worship. This knowledge was then passed down from generation to generation. The hereditary Pawnee chiefs kept the star bundle hanging from a buffalo-hair rope in the sacred, western portion of their lodges—the section that was associated with the evening star and reserved for priests during the performance of ceremonies.

A buffalo skull rests on the east-facing altar as a symbolic reminder of the great importance of the animal to the Pawnee Indians.

ALTAR

EAST

Bundles of cotton-wood tree trunks, used for building, rest against the tunnel-like entryway to a Pawnee lodge in Nebraska in 1871. The spacious lodges—up to 60 feet in diameter— were built with the labor of the inhabit-ants and blessed by a priest, who re-minded the people that the houses were built in the im-age of the sky vault raised by the gods.

A great circle of Blackfoot tipis, photographed in 1896 when the tribe assembled for its annual Sun Dance, measures more than one mile in circumference. At the climactic stage of the long Sun Dance ceremony, the painted medicine tipis formed a sacred circle within the larger ring of shelters.

THE ETERNAL RING
OF THE PLAINS PEOPLE

Wherever they roamed, the nomadic peoples of the prairie carried their world with them in the form of the tipi. As a microcosm of the universe, its circular ground plan echoed not only the larger camp circle to which the shelter belonged, as shown above, but also the encompassing disk of the earth, stretched out beneath the heavens. The floor of the tipi represented the earth and the walls the sky, while the poles were seen as pathways between the two realms, linking the human inhabitants to Wa-

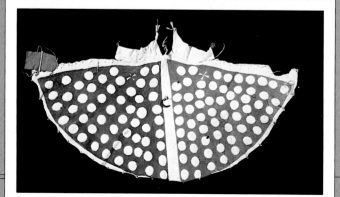

kan Tanka, the Great Mystery, above.

The tipi was generally pitched facing east, both in obeisance to the rising sun and to keep the entrance away from the prevailing winds. Inside, be-

hind the firepit and opposite the doorway, a portion of sod was removed and the earth brushed smooth to create a family altar—a "square of mellowed earth" to the Sioux—where fragrant grasses were burned as offerings in smoke to the spirits above.

Traditionally made of buffalo skin, tipi covers were battered by wind, dust, rain, and constant hauling from one camp to another, and had to be replaced as often as once a year. They were usually left undecorated, but every

village contained a number of painted medicine tipis. These were used by the Indians for special ceremonies to guard against ill fortune and to bring success in battle or the hunt.

The possession of these ceremonial tipis conferred honor but also obliged the owner to pay scrupulous attention to ritual form and to take special care of the tipi's cover. When the time came for one of them to be replaced, its design was painted on a new hide, and the old one was burned. The rights to the design used and the responsibility for the powerful medicine that was associated with it were handed down from generation to generation.

In this model of a Kiowa tipi cover (far left), the circles symbolize stars against the dark backdrop of the sky. The two crosses at the top represent the morning star, which was situated so as to face east above the entrance when the flaps were joined.

An Arapaho named Little Big Mouth sits in front of his hide-covered tipi. Long wooden pins close the front seam of the tent.

ACKNOWLEDGMENTS

The editors wish to thank the following for their valuable assistance in the preparation of this volume:

In Germany:
Munich—Jean-Loup Rousselot, Staatliches Museum für Völkerkunde. Stuttgart—Ursula Didoni, Axel Schulze-Thulin, Linden-Museum Stuttgart.

In the United States:
Arizona: Paradise Valley—Joe Ben, Jr.
California: Eureka—Maria and Amos Tripp. Redding—Philip McDonald, U.S. Forest Service. San Pedro—Dr. Pete Lee, Los Angeles Maritime Museum. Trinidad—Axel Lindgren; Jerome J. Simone, United Indian Health Services.
Illinois: Chicago—Mary Ann Bloom, Nina Cummings, Field Museum; Harvey Markowitz, D'Arcy McNickle Center, Newberry Library.
Indiana: Fort Wayne—W. Jayne Baker. Leo—Wendy Bloom.
Montana: Wolf Point—Danna Clark Runsabove.
New Mexico: Santa Fe—Eunice Kahn, Wheelwright Museum of the American Indian.
North Carolina: Cherokee—Mary U. Chiltoskey.
Pennsylvania: Philadelphia—Lucy Williams, University Museum, University of Pennsylvania.
South Dakota: Mobridge—Kevin Locke.
Washington, D.C.: Nicholas J. Parella, Felicia Pickering, Smithsonian Institution.
Washington State: Seattle—Rebecca Andrews, The Burke Museum, University of Washington; Richard H. Engeman, Sandra Kroupa, Gary L. Menges, Carla Rickerson, University of Washington Libraries; Vie Hilbert; Sari Ott, Stan Shockey, University of Washington.
Wyoming: Cody—Elizabeth Holmes, Buffalo Bill Historic Center.

BIBLIOGRAPHY

BOOKS

Bahr, Donald M., et al., *Piman Shamanism and Staying Sickness.* Tucson: University of Arizona Press, 1974.

Bahti, Tom, *Southwestern Indian Ceremonials.* Las Vegas, Nev.: KC Publications, 1970.

Bancroft-Hunt, Norman, *The Indians of the Great Plains.* New York: Peter Bedrick Books, 1989.

Beck, Peggy V., Anna Lee Walters, and Nia Francisco, *The Sacred Ways of Knowledge, Sources of Life.* Tsaile, Ariz.: Navajo Community College Press, 1992.

Bierhorst, John, *The Mythology of North America.* New York: William Morrow, 1985.

Billard, Jules B., ed., *The World of the American Indian.* Washington, D.C.: National Geographic Society, 1979.

Boas, Franz, *The Social Organization and the Secret Societies of the Kwakiutl Indians.* Washington, D.C.: Government Printing Office, 1897.

Brown, Joseph Epes, ed., *The Sacred Pipe: Black Elk's Account of the Seven Rites of the Oglala Sioux.* Norman: University of Oklahoma Press, 1953.

Bruchac, Joseph, *Iroquois Stories: Heroes and Heroines, Monsters and Magic.* Freedom, Calif.: Crossing Press, 1985.

Burch, Ernest S., Jr., *The Eskimos.* London: Macdonald & Co, 1988.

Burland, Cottie, *North American Indian Mythology.* New York: Peter Bedrick Books, 1985.

Capps, Benjamin, and the Editors of Time-Life Books:
The Great Chiefs (The Old West series). Alexandria, Va.: Time-Life Books, 1975.
The Indians (The Old West series). Alexandria, Va.: Time-Life Books, 1973.

Campbell, Joseph, *The Way of the Animal Powers: Mythologies of the Primitive Hunters and Gatherers.* Vol. 1, Part 1 of *Historical Atlas of World Mythology.* New York: Harper & Row, 1988.

Cavendish, Richard, ed., *Man, Myth & Magic: The Illustrated Encyclopedia of Mythology, Religion and the Unknown.* New York: Marshall Cavendish, 1985.

Chamberlain, Von Del, *When Stars Came Down To Earth: Cosmology of the Skidi Pawnee Indians of North America.* Los Altos, Calif.: Ballena Press, 1982.

Conn, Richard, *Circles of the World: Traditional Art of the Plains Indians.* Denver: Denver Art Museum, 1982.

Culin, Stewart, *Games of the North American Indians.* New York: Dover Publications, 1975.

Cushing, Frank Hamilton, *Zuni Folk Tales.* Tucson: University of Arizona Press, 1988 (reprint of 1931 edition).

Dempsey, Hugh A., *Treasures of the Glenbow Museum.* Calgary, Alberta: Paperworks Press, 1991.

The Desert Realm: Lands of Majesty and Mystery. Washington, D.C.: National Geographic Society, 1982.

Dockstader, Frederick J., *The Kachina and the White Man: The Influences of White Culture on the Hopi Kachina Religion.* Albuquerque: University of New Mexico Press, 1985.

Edmonds, Margot, and Ella E. Clark, *Voices of the Winds: Native American Legends.* New York: Facts On File, 1989.

Emanuels, George, *California Indians: An Illustrated Guide.* Walnut Creek, Calif.: Diablo Books, 1991.

Erdoes, Richard, and Alfonso Ortiz, eds., *American Indian Myths and Legends.* New York: Pantheon Books, 1984.

Ewing, Douglas C., *Pleasing the Spirits: A Catalogue of a Collection of American Indian Art.* New York: Ghylen Press, 1982.

Fane, Diana, Ira Jacknis, and Lise M. Breen, *Objects of Myth and Memory.* New York: Brooklyn Museum, 1991.

Faris, James C., *The Nightway: A History and a History of Documentation of a Navajo Ceremonial.* Albuquerque: University of New Mexico Press, 1990.

Fenton, William N., *The False Faces of the Iroquois.* Norman: University of Oklahoma Press, 1987.

Fire, John/Lame Deer, and Richard Erdoes, *Lame Deer: Seeker of Visions.* New York: Simon and Schuster, 1972.

Fitzhugh, William W., and Susan A. Kaplan, *Inua: Spirit World of the Bering Sea Eskimo.* Washington, D.C.: Smithsonian Institution Press, 1982.

Gill, Sam D.:
Native American Religions: An Introduction. Belmont, Calif.: Wadsworth Publishing, 1982.
Native American Traditions: Sources and Interpretations. Belmont, Calif.: Wadsworth Publishing, 1983.

Gray, John S., *Centennial Campaign: The Sioux War of 1876.* Norman: University of Oklahoma Press, 1976.

Halifax, Joan, *Shaman: The Wounded Healer.* New York: Crossroad Publishing, 1982.

Hamel, Paul B., and Mary U. Chiltoskey, *Cherokee Plants: Their Uses—A 400 Year History.* Sylva, N.C.: Herald Publishing, 1975.

Harrington, M. R., *Religion and Ceremonies of the Lenape.* New York: Museum of the American Indian, Heye Foundation, 1921.

Hawthorn, Audrey, *Kwakiutl Art.* Vancouver, British Columbia: Douglas & McIntyre, 1988.

Heizer, Robert F., and Albert B. Elsasser, *The Natural World of the California Indians.* Berkeley: University of California Press, 1980.

Heizer, Robert F., and M. A. Whipple, *The California Indians.* Berkeley: University of California Press, 1971.

Hodge, Frederick Webb, ed., *Handbook of American Indians North of Mexico.* Parts 1 and 2. New York: Rowman and Littlefield, 1971.

Hofsinde, Robert (Gray-Wolf), *The Indian Medicine Man.* New York: William Morrow, 1966.

Holm, Bill:
The Art and Times of Willie Seaweed. Seattle: University of Washington Press, 1983.
Crooked Beak of Heaven: Masks and Other Ceremonial Art of the Northwest Coast. Seattle: University of Washington Press, 1972.
Spirit and Ancestor: A Century of Northwest Coast Indian Art at the Burke Museum. Seattle: University of Washington Press, 1987.

Horse Capture, George P., *Powwow.* Cody, Wyo.: Buffalo Bill Historical Center, 1989.

Hoxie, Frederick E., *The Crow.* New York, Chelsea House Publishers, 1989.

Hudson, Charles M., ed., *Black Drink: A Native American Tea.* Athens: University of Georgia Press, 1979.

Hultkrantz, Åke, *Belief and Worship in Native North America.* Ed. by Christopher Vecsey. Syracuse, N.Y.: Syracuse University Press, 1981.

Hutchens, Alma R., *Indian Herbalogy of North America.* Boston: Shambhala, 1991.

Jett, Stephen C., and Virginia E. Spencer, *Navajo Architecture: Forms, History, Distributions.* Tucson: University of Arizona Press, 1981.

Johnston, Basil, *Ojibway Ceremonies.* Toronto: McClelland and Stewart, 1982.

Jonaitis, Aldona, *From the Land of the Totem Poles: The Northwest Coast Indian Art Collection at the American Museum of Natural History.* New York: American Museum of Natural History, 1988.

Jonaitis, Aldona, ed., *Chiefly Feasts: The Enduring Kwakiutl Potlatch.* Seattle: University of Washington Press, 1991.

Kehoe, Alice Beck, *North American Indians: A Comprehensive Account.* Englewood Cliffs, N.J.: Prentice-Hall, 1981.

Kroeber, Alfred Lewis:
Handbook of the Indians of California. Washington, D.C.: Government Printing Office, 1925.
Yurok Myths. Berkeley: University of California Press, 1976.

La Barre, Weston, *The Peyote Cult.* Hamden, Conn.: Archon Books, 1975.

Lowie, Robert H.:
The Crow Indians. Lincoln: University of Nebraska Press, 1963.
Indians of the Plains. Lincoln: University of Nebraska Press, 1982.

MacDonald, George F., *Haida Monumental Art: Villages of the Queen Charlotte Islands.* Vancouver: University of British Columbia Press, 1983.

Maclagan, David, *Creation Myths: Man's Introduction to the World.* New York: Thames and Hudson, 1977.

Mails, Thomas E., *The Mystic Warriors of the Plains.* New York: Mallard Press, 1991.

Malin, Edward, *A World of Faces: Masks of the Northwest Coast Indians.* Portland, Oreg.: Timber Press, 1978.

Marriott, Alice, and Carol K. Rachlin, *Peyote.* New York: Thomas Y. Crowell, 1971.

Mathews, Zena Pearlstone, *Symbol and Substance in American Indian Art.* New York: Metropolitan Museum of Art, 1984.

Matthews, Washington, *The Night Chant: A Navaho Ceremony.* Vol. 6 of *Memoirs of the American Museum of Natural History.* New York: Knickerbocker Press, 1902.

Maxwell, James A., ed., *America's Fascinating Indian Heritage.* Pleasantville, N.Y.: The Reader's Digest Association, 1978.

Merriam, C. Hart, *Studies of California Indians.* Berkeley: University of California Press, 1955.

Miller, Jay, ed., *Mourning Dove: A Salishan Autobiography.* Lincoln: University of Nebraska Press, 1990.

Morgan, Lewis H., *Houses and House-Life of the American Aborigines.* Chicago: University of Chicago Press, 1969.

Murie, James R., *Ceremonies of the Pawnee.* Ed. by Douglas R. Parks. Lincoln: University of Nebraska Press, 1981.

Nabokov, Peter, and Robert Easton, *Native American Architecture.* New York: Oxford University Press, 1989.

Neihardt, John G., *Black Elk Speaks: Being the Life Story of a Holy Man of the Ogalala Sioux.* New York: William Morrow, 1932.

Nelson, Edward William, *The Eskimo about Bering Strait.* Washington, D.C.: Smithsonian Institution Press, 1983.

Newcomb, Franc Johnson, Stanley Fishler, and Mary C. Wheelwright, *A Study of Navajo Symbolism.* New York: Kraus Reprint Corporation, 1968 (reprint of 1956 edition).

Ortiz, Alfonso, *The Tewa World: Space, Time, Being, and Becoming in a Pueblo Society.* Chicago: University of Chicago Press, 1969.

Ortiz, Alfonso, ed., *Southwest.* Vol. 9 of *Handbook of North American Indians.* Washington, D.C.: Smithsonian Institution, 1979.

Paper, Jordan, *Offering Smoke: The Sacred Pipe and Native American Religion.* Edmonton: The University of Alberta Press, 1989.

Peterson, Lee Allen, *A Field Guide to Edible Wild Plants: Eastern and Central North America.* Boston: Houghton Mifflin, 1977.

Powers, Stephen, *Tribes of California.* Washington, D.C.: Government Printing Office, 1877.

Reichard, Gladys A., *Navaho Religion: A Study of Symbolism.* New York: Pantheon Books, 1963.

Rohner, Ronald P., and Evelyn C. Rohner, *The Kwakiutl: Indians of British Columbia.* New York: Holt, Rinehart and Winston, 1970.

Ruoff, A. LaVonne Brown, *Literatures of the American Indian.* Ed. by Frank W. Porter, III. New York: Chelsea House Publishers, 1991.

Schaafsma, Polly, *Indian Rock Art of the Southwest.* Santa Fe, N.Mex.: School of American Research, 1980.

Speck, Frank Gouldsmith, *The Delaware Indian Big House Ceremony.* New York: AMS Press, 1981.

Spence, Lewis, *The Myths of the North American Indians.* New York: Dover Publications, 1989.

The Spirit Sings: Artistic Traditions of Canada's First Peoples. Toronto: McClelland and Stewart, 1987.

Standing Bear, Chief, *Land of the Spotted Eagle.* Boston: Houghton Mifflin, 1933.

Stewart, Omer C., *Peyote Religion: A History.* Norman: University of Oklahoma Press, 1987.

Stewart, Tyrone, Frederick Dockstader, and Barton Wright, *The Year of the Hopi: Paintings and Photographs by Joseph Mora, 1904-06.* New York: Rizzoli, 1979.

Tedlock, Dennis, and Barbara Tedlock, eds., *Teachings from the American Earth: Indian Religion and Philosophy.* New York: Liveright, 1975.

Thompson, Stith, *Tales of the North American Indians.* Bloomington: Indiana University Press, 1966.

Torrence, Gaylord, and Robert Hobbs, *Art of the Red Earth People: The Mesquakie of Iowa.* Iowa City: University of Iowa Museum of Art, 1989.

Trenton, Patricia, and Patrick T. Houlihan, *Native Americans: Five Centuries of Changing Images.* New York: Harry N. Abrams, 1989.

Tyler, Hamilton A., *Pueblo Birds and Myths.* Flagstaff, Ariz.: Northland Publishing, 1991.

Underhill, Ruth M.:
Papago Indian Religion. New York: AMS Press, 1969.
Red Man's Religion: Beliefs and Practices of the Indians North of Mexico. Chicago: University of Chicago Press, 1965.

Waldman, Carl:
Atlas of the North American Indian. New York: Facts On File Publications, 1985.
Encyclopedia of Native American Tribes. New York: Facts on File Publications, 1988.

Walters, Anna Lee, *The Spirit of Native America: Beauty and Mysticism in American Indian Art.* San Francisco: Chronicle Books, 1989.

Waters, Frank, *Masked Gods: Navajo and Pueblo Ceremonialism.* Athens, Ohio: Swallow Press, 1989.

Wardwell, Allen, *Objects of Bright Pride: Northwest Coast Indian Art from the American Museum of Natural History.* New York: American Federation of Arts, 1988.

Weltfish, Gene, *The Lost Universe.* New York: Basic Books, 1965.

Weslager, C. A., *Magic Medicines of the Indians.* Somerset, N.J.: Middle Atlantic Press, 1973.

Witthoft, John, *Green Corn Ceremonialism in the Eastern Woodlands.* Ann Arbor: University of Michigan Press, 1949.

Wright, Barton, *Hopi Kachinas: The Complete Guide to Collecting Kachina Dolls.* Flagstaff, Ariz.: Northland Publishing, 1977.

Wyman, Leland C., *Southwest Indian Drypainting.* Albuquerque: University of New Mexico Press, 1983.

PERIODICALS

McCoy, Ronald:
"Circles of Power," *Plateau* (Flagstaff, Ariz.), 1984.
"Summoning the Gods: Sandpainting in the Native American Southwest," *Plateau* (Flagstaff, Ariz.), 1988.

Ortiz, Alfonso, "Origins," *National Geographic,* October 1991.

OTHER SOURCES

Blackman, Margaret S., "Window on the Past: The Photographic Ethnohistory of the Northern and Kaigani Haida." *National Museum of Man Mercury Series,* Canadian Ethnology Service Paper #74. Ottawa (Ontario): 1981.

PICTURE CREDITS

Cover: Courtesy of the Royal Ontario Museum, Toronto. 6: © Michael Crummett. 8: Map by Maryland CartoGraphics, Inc. 9: Photo by Edward S. Curtis, Library of Congress (LC-USZ62-49150). 10, 11: C. M. Dixon, Canterbury, Kent. 12, 13: Tom Galliher, Fort Wayne, Indiana. 15: Library of Congress (LC-USZ62-97091); Smithsonian Institution, neg. #1008. 16: Special Collections Division, University of Washington Libraries, photo by Edward S. Curtis, photo #NA472; State Historical Society of North Dakota. 17: Photo by Grace Nicholson, courtesy National Museum of the American Indian, Smithsonian Institution, neg. #18982; Smithsonian Institution, neg. #2777. 18: Neg. #41618, courtesy Department Library Services, American Museum of Natural History, New York; State Historical Society of North Dakota, neg. #A-1007, photo by R. L. Beatie. 20, 21: Smithsonian Institution, neg. #56747—Schenck & Schenck, courtesy Southwest Museum and Axel Lindgren, on loan to the Maritime Museum, Los Angeles; © Leonard L. Stevens. 22, 23: Siskiyou County Historical Society; Vern Korb, Shenandoah Films; © Alan Dismuke (2). 24: Denver Art Museum, acquisition #1959.143. 26, 27: © Leon C. Yost. 28, 29: Tom Galliher, all courtesy Kevin Locke, except drum made by Barbara Weaving Fire. 30: Werner Forman Archive, London/Provincial Museum, Victoria, British Columbia—Werner Forman Archive, London/National Museum of Man, Ottawa, Ontario. 31: Smithsonian Institution, neg. #2374. 33: Art by Greg Harlin of Stansbury, Ronsaville, Wood Inc.—Special Collections Division, University of Washington Libraries, photo by Edward S. Curtis, photo #NA133. 35: George P. Horse Capture, courtesy Danna Clark Runs-above; Danna Clark Runsabove. 36, 37: Royal British Columbia Museum, Victoria, British Columbia, cat. #16460, courtesy University of Washington Press; Smithsonian Institution, neg. #86-2842. 38: Trans. #4528(2), photo by Lynton Gardiner, courtesy Department Library Services, American Museum of Natural History, New York. 39: Trans. #4549(2), photo by Lynton Gardiner, courtesy Department Library Services, American Museum of Natural History, New York. 40: Trans. #4512(2), photo by Lynton Gardiner, courtesy Department Library Services, American Museum of Natural History, New York. 41: W. McLennan, University of British Columbia Museum of Anthropology, Vancouver, British Columbia. 42: Trans. #4519(2), photo by Lynton Gardiner, courtesy Department of Library Services, American Museum of Natural History, New York. 43: Courtesy of the Thomas Burke Memorial Washington State Museum, cat. #2.5E1605, photo by Eduardo Calderón—courtesy of the Thomas Burke Memorial Washington State Museum, cat. #25.0/215, photo by Eduardo Calderón. 44, 45: Courtesy Glenbow Museum, Calgary, Alberta, Canada, cat. #R180.219, photo by Anita Dammer (2). 46: Courtesy of the Thomas Burke Memorial Washington State Museum, cat. #1-1450, photo by Eduardo Calderón. 47: Courtesy of the Thomas Burke

Memorial Washington State Museum, cat. #1-1451, photo by Eduardo Calderón. 48: © Stephen Trimble. 50, 51: E. I. Couse, Couse Family Archives, Couse Enterprises Ltd. 52, 53: Schenck & Schenck, courtesy Southwest Museum, Los Angeles (3). 54: Smithsonian Institution, neg. #43114A. 56: Courtesy of the Thomas Burke Memorial Washington State Museum, cat. #117A, photo by Eduardo Calderón. 57: Photo by Larry Sherer, Department of Anthropology, Smithsonian Institution, cat. #38732. 58: Parrot, The Brooklyn Museum #03.325 3275, Museum Expedition 1908, Museum Collection Fund. 60, 61: Photo by T. Harman Parkhurst, courtesy Museum of New Mexico, Santa Fe, neg. #2258. 62: Linden-Museum Stuttgart, Collection Paul, Stuttgart, Germany, photo by Ursula Didoni. 63: Smithsonian Institution, cat. #245023. 64: Courtesy of the Thomas Burke Memorial Washington State Museum, cat. #2.5E604, photo by Eduardo Calderón. 65: National Museum of American Art, Washington, D.C./Art Resource, New York. 66: Werner Forman Archive, London/Glenbow Museum, Calgary, Alberta, Canada. 67: © Marcia Keegan. 68, 69: National Museum of American Art, Washington, D.C./Art Resource, New York. 70: Field Museum of Natural History, Chicago, trans. #A111827c. 71: Photo by Hillel Burger, Peabody Museum, Harvard University, #T918. 72, 73: Natalie B. Fobes/Allstock. 74: Phoebe Apperson Hearst Museum of Anthropology, University of California at Berkeley. 77: Werner Forman Archive, London/Museum für Völkerkunde, Berlin. 78: Denver Art Museum, acquisition #1948.161. 79: Buffalo Bill Historical Center, Cody, Wyoming—Colter Bay Indian Arts Museum, Grand Teton National Park, Moose, Wyoming. 80, 81: Neg. #2A 12701, courtesy Department Library Services, American Museum of Natural History, New York—Otto Nelson, courtesy Denver Art Museum, acquisition #1938.160,161—Otto Nelson, courtesy Denver Art Museum, acquisition #1940.50; Head Plume, The Brooklyn Museum #08.491.8812, Museum Expedition 1908, Museum Collection Fund. 82, 83: University Museum, University of Pennsylvania, #T4-367c2(2)—#T4-370c2; #T4-368c2; #T4-369c2. 84, 85: Courtesy Glenbow Museum, Calgary, Alberta, Canada, AF 1671—Fred E. Miller, courtesy Nancy F. O'Connor, © Carnan Vidfilm, Inc. 87: © Michael Crummett (2). 90: Betty Soleman Webber Collection, Ottumwa, Iowa—courtesy Mr. and Mrs. Larry Frank—Detroit Institute of Arts. 92, 93: Fred E. Miller, courtesy Nancy F. O'Connor, © Carnan Vidfilm, Inc. 94, 95: © Marcia Keegan. 96: Rochester Museum and Science Center, Rochester, New York (.MR721). 97: Trans. #50.1/4312, photo by E. Mortenson, American Museum of Natural History, New York. 98, 99: Smithsonian Institution, neg. #1824-D. 101: Library of Congress (LC-USZ62-101181). 102: © Martha Cooper/Peter Arnold, Inc. 104: Trans. #50.1/5466, American Museum of Natural History, New York. 106, 107: Larry Sherer, Botannical Library, National Museum of Natural History, Smithsonian Institution, Washington, D.C. (4). 108, 109: Denver Art Museum, photo by Lloyd Rule, acquisition #1951.110; courtesy National Museum of the American Indian, Smithsonian Institution, cat. #4748. 111: Smithsonian Institution, neg. #55490. 113: Smithsonian Institution, neg. #86-4103. 114, 115: Courtesy Wheelwright Mu-

seum of the American Indian (P3A-#4A); (P4-#4A). 116, 117: Courtesy Wheelwright Museum of the American Indian (P20-#6); (P1A-#8). 118, 119: © Jerry Jacka. 120: Smithsonian Institution, neg. #77-2861. 122, 123: © Michael Crummett. 124: Smithsonian Institution, neg. #3303-c/e; Western Historical Manuscript Collection, University of Missouri. 126, 127: Linden-Museum Stuttgart, Collection Paul, Stuttgart, Germany, photo by Ursula Didoni; National Museum of American Art, Washington, D.C./Art Resource, New York. 129: Nebraska State Historical Society. 130, 131: Art by Greg Harlin of Stansbury, Ronsaville, Wood Inc. (6)—Field Museum of Natural History, Chicago, neg. #A111351c; National Museum of the American Indian, Smithsonian Institution, cat. #2473. 132, 133: Courtesy National Museum of the American Indian, Smithsonian Institution, trans. #2656; trans. #3771. 134: Field Museum of Natural History, Chicago, neg. #16231c. 135: Smithsonian Institution, neg. #476-A-13. 137: Courtesy of the Thomas Burke Memorial Washington State Museum—courtesy of the Thomas Burke Memorial Washington State Museum, cat. #1-11392, photo by Eduardo Calderón. 138: Werner Forman Archive, London/Provincial Museum, Victoria, British Columbia—Werner Forman Archive, London; trans. #3820, photo by Stephen S. Myers, American Museum of Natural History, New York. 139: Trans. #3818, photo by Stephen S. Myers, American Museum of Natural History, New York. 140: Courtesy of the Thomas Burke Memorial Washington State Museum, cat. #1-2194, photo by Eduardo Calderón—courtesy of the Thomas Burke Memorial Washington State Museum, cat. #2067, photo by Eduardo Calderón—courtesy of the Thomas Burke Memorial Washington State Museum, cat. #1971, photo by Eduardo Calderón. 142, 143: Courtesy National Museum of the American Indian, Smithsonian Institution, neg. #2657—Schoharie Museum of the Iroquois Indian, #461.1. 144: Smithsonian Institution, neg. #55298. 145: National Museum of the American Indian, Smithsonian Institution, trans. #2336. 147: Smithsonian Institution, neg. #2372-C-19. 148, 149: Smithsonian Institution, neg. #52550; photo by Hillel Burger, Peabody Museum, Harvard University, T1248. 150: Denver Art Museum, acquisition #1970.519-32. 151: National Museum of American Art, Washington, D.C./Art Resource, New York. 153: Smithsonian Institution, neg. #1044-B—neg. #1042. 154, 155: © Stephen Trimble. 156, 157: Southwest Museum, Los Angeles, photo by Walter McClintock. 158: Royal British Columbia Museum, Victoria, British Columbia (PN 701). 159: Art by Greg Harlin of Stansbury, Ronsaville, Wood Inc. 160, 161: Courtesy Colorado Historical Society, neg. #F15,887; art by Greg Harlin of Stansbury, Ronsaville, Wood Inc. 162, 163: Smithsonian Institution, neg. #83-3012; Library of Congress (206653)—art by Greg Harlin of Stansbury, Ronsaville, Wood Inc. 164, 165: Art by Greg Harlin of Stansbury, Ronsaville, Wood Inc. (2); courtesy National Museum of the American Indian, Smithsonian Institution, neg. #2876; inset trans. #4746. 166, 167: Art by Greg Harlin of Stansbury, Ronsaville, Wood Inc.; Smithsonian Institution, neg. #1248. 168, 169: Southwest Museum, Los Angeles, photo by Walter McClintock—Smithsonian Institution, cat. #229893; neg. #1448-D-2.